The Flexible Budget Blueprint

A Guide to Fluid Financial Planning

Isabella S. Lee

Xspurts.com

A New Zealand Designed Product

Other Versions Available

Why limit yourself to just one format?

This book is now available in physical, digital, and audiobook options.

Choose the way you love to read and dive into the story today. You won't regret it!

Digital ISBN: 9781776848058
Physical ISBN: 9781776846962
Audio ISBN:

To obtain a different format of this book at a discounted price, please get in touch with us at:

http://isbn.xspurts.com/

Contents

Have Questions / Comments?

This book was designed to cover as much information as possible, but I know I have probably missed something, or some new amazing discovery has just come out.

If you notice something missing or have a question that I failed to answer, please get in touch and let me know. If I can, I will email you an answer and also update the book so others can also benefit from it.

Thanks For Being Awesome :)

Submit Your Questions / Comments At:

https://questions.xspurts.com

Get Free Stuff

We love writing and have produced a huge number of books.

For being one of our amazing readers, we would love to offer you more books we have created, 100% free.

To claim this limited time special offer, simply go to the site below and enter your name and email address.

You will then receive loads (as we love our readers so much :) of our great books, content and audio direct to your email account, 100% free!

Get Loads of FREE Stuff at:

https://free.xspurts.com

Chapter One

Understanding Flexible Budgeting

Budgeting is a fundamental aspect of financial management for organizations. It involves planning and allocating resources to achieve business objectives. Traditional budgeting approaches often rely on fixed targets and assumptions, which may not effectively address the dynamic nature of today's business environment. In contrast, flexible budgeting offers a more adaptive and responsive approach that allows organizations to adjust their financial plans based on changing circumstances. Below we will explore the concept of flexible budgeting, its benefits, and its application in organizations.

What is Flexible Budgeting?

Flexible budgeting, also known as variable budgeting or dynamic budgeting, is a budgeting approach that allows for adjustments to financial plans in response to changes in activity levels, revenues, or costs. Unlike traditional static budgets, which are fixed for a specific period, flexible budgets are designed to accommodate fluctuations in business conditions. By incorporating flexibility into the budgeting process, organizations can make more accurate projections, monitor performance effectively, and respond promptly to deviations from the initial plan.

The Benefits of Flexible Budgeting:

Flexible budgeting offers several benefits that contribute to better financial management and decision, making within organizations:

a) Enhanced Accuracy: Flexible budgets take into account the variability of revenues and costs based on different activity levels. This approach provides a more realistic representation of expected financial performance, allowing organizations to make more accurate forecasts and projections.

b) Improved Performance Evaluation: With flexible budgets, organizations can compare actual results against budgeted targets at various activity levels. This analysis provides insights into the efficiency and effectiveness of resource utilization, enabling better performance evaluation and identification of areas for improvement.

c) Responsive Decision, Making: In a dynamic business environment, organizations need to be agile in responding to changes. Flexible budgets enable management to assess the financial impact of alternative courses of action and make informed decisions based on the most up, to, date information.

d) Cost Control: Flexible budgeting allows organizations to monitor and control costs more effectively. By analyzing cost behavior at different activity levels, organizations can identify cost drivers, optimize resource allocation, and implement cost, saving measures more efficiently.

e) Resource Allocation: Flexible budgets help organizations allocate resources more efficiently by considering the changing needs of different activities or departments. This approach ensures that resources are allocated based on the actual requirements, leading to better utilization and optimization of available resources.

Implementing Flexible Budgeting:

Implementing flexible budgeting requires careful planning and execution. Here are some key steps to consider:

a) Data Collection and Analysis: Organizations need to gather historical data on revenues and costs, as well as information on the factors that influence these variables. Analyzing the historical data helps identify patterns, trends, and relationships, which can inform the development of a flexible budget model.

b) Activity, Based Budgeting: Flexible budgets are typically based on activity levels or cost drivers. Organizations need to identify the key activities or cost drivers that impact their financial performance and determine how changes in these variables affect revenues and costs.

c) Setting Activity Levels: Activity levels serve as a basis for developing the flexible budget. Organizations need to set realistic activity level targets based on market conditions, customer demand, and internal capabilities. These targets should reflect the expected range of activity levels that the organization may experience.

d) Establishing Cost Relationships: Organizations need to establish the relationships between activity levels and costs. This involves analyzing historical cost data to determine how costs change as activity levels fluctuate. This information is crucial for building the cost structure of the flexible budget.

e) Monitoring and Evaluation: Once the flexible budget is in place, organizations need to regularly monitor actual performance against the budgeted targets. Any deviations from the plan should be analyzed and understood to identify the underlying causes and take appropriate corrective actions.

What is a Flexible Budget?

A Flexible Budget: Adapting to Changing Realities

Budgeting is a crucial financial management tool used by organizations to plan and control their expenses and revenues. It provides a roadmap for achieving financial objectives and ensures efficient resource allocation. However, traditional budgeting approaches often fall short in addressing the dynamic nature of businesses and the uncertainties they face. This is where a flexible budget comes into play. Below we will explore the concept of a flexible budget, its advantages, and its role in enabling organizations to adapt to changing realities.

Defining a Flexible Budget:

A flexible budget is a financial plan that adjusts to changes in activity levels, revenues, and costs. Unlike static budgets that are fixed for a specific period, a flexible budget allows organizations to modify their financial plans to reflect the actual level of business activity. It is designed to be responsive and adaptable, enabling organizations to make more accurate forecasts and better assess their financial performance.

Key Features and Components:

A flexible budget consists of several key features and components:

a) Activity Levels: The flexible budget considers various activity levels or volume drivers, such as units produced, sales volume, or service hours. These activity levels serve as the basis for estimating revenues and costs at different levels of business activity.

b) Revenue Projections: The flexible budget incorporates revenue projections that correspond to each activity level. By analyzing historical data and market conditions, organizations can estimate the expected revenue based on the volume of business activity.

c) Variable Costs: Variable costs are expenses that change in direct proportion to changes in activity levels. Examples include direct materials, direct labor, and variable overhead costs. The flexible budget accounts for these variable costs and adjusts them accordingly as activity levels change.

d) Fixed Costs: Fixed costs remain constant regardless of changes in activity levels. They include expenses such as rent, insurance, and salaries. While fixed costs do not change with activity levels, they are still included in the flexible budget to provide a complete picture of overall costs.

e) Semi, variable Costs: Semi, variable costs have both fixed and variable components. They include expenses such as utilities, maintenance, and equipment depreciation. The flexible budget takes into account the variable portion of these costs based on activity levels.

Advantages of a Flexible Budget:

A flexible budget offers several advantages that can enhance financial planning and decision, making within organizations:

a) Accurate Performance Evaluation: By incorporating activity levels and variable costs, a flexible budget provides a more accurate assessment of performance. Organizations can compare actual results with the budgeted amounts at different activity levels, enabling them to identify deviations and take appropriate corrective actions.

b) Better Cost Control: With a flexible budget, organizations can closely monitor and control costs by analyzing their behavior at various activity levels. This allows for more effective cost management and optimization of resource allocation.

c) Improved Decision, Making: A flexible budget provides organizations with the ability to evaluate the financial impact of alternative courses of action. This enables informed decision, making and helps identify the most cost, effective strategies.

d) Adaptability to Changing Conditions: In a dynamic business environment, a flexible budget allows organizations to respond quickly to changes in market conditions, customer demand, or internal factors. It provides the necessary flexibility to adjust financial plans and align them with current realities.

e) Enhanced Forecasting: By considering different activity levels, a flexible budget enables organizations to make more accurate revenue and cost projections. This leads to more reliable financial forecasts, aiding in strategic planning and resource allocation.

Implementing a Flexible Budget:

Implementing a flexible budget requires careful planning and execution. Here are some key steps to consider:

a) Identify Key Activity Drivers: Organizations need to identify the primary drivers of their business activities. This could be units produced, sales volume, or any other relevant factor that affects revenues and costs.

The Importance of Flexibility in Budgeting

Budgeting is a fundamental aspect of financial management for individuals, businesses, and organizations. It involves setting financial goals, estimating revenues and expenses, and allocating resources accordingly. While budgeting provides a roadmap for financial success, rigid and inflexible budgeting approaches can hinder an organization's ability to adapt to changing circumstances. Below we will explore the importance of flexibility in budgeting and its role in promoting financial resilience and agility.

Responding to Uncertainty:

The business landscape is characterized by uncertainty, with factors such as economic fluctuations, market dynamics, and technological advancements constantly reshaping the operating environment. A flexible budget allows organizations to navigate these uncertainties by incorporating contingency plans and considering different scenarios. It enables proactive decision, making and helps organizations respond swiftly to unforeseen challenges or opportunities.

Adapting to Changing Priorities:

In today's fast, paced world, priorities and strategies can shift rapidly. Organizations need the flexibility to reallocate resources and adjust their financial plans accordingly. By embracing flexible budgeting, organizations can align their financial resources with evolving priorities, ensuring that funds are allocated to initiatives that drive growth and deliver the most value. This adaptability promotes strategic agility and supports the achievement of organizational goals.

Capitalizing on Market Opportunities:

Market opportunities often arise unexpectedly, requiring organizations to act swiftly to capitalize on them. A flexible budget enables organizations to seize these opportunities by allocating the necessary resources in a timely manner. Whether it's launching a new product, expanding into new markets, or investing in research and development, flexibility in budgeting ensures that organizations can make informed financial decisions and seize competitive advantages.

Managing Variability in Revenues and Costs:

Revenues and costs are rarely constant, and organizations must account for this variability in their budgeting process. Flexible budgeting allows for adjustments to revenue and cost projections based on changing market conditions, customer demand, or internal factors. It provides organizations with a more accurate picture of their financial position and empowers them to manage their resources effectively.

Enhancing Decision, Making:

A flexible budget provides decision, makers with valuable insights into the financial implications of different courses of action. It enables them to evaluate the financial impact of alternative scenarios and make informed choices. With the ability to assess the consequences of various decisions, organizations can optimize their resource allocation, identify cost, saving opportunities, and make strategic investments that align with their objectives.

Promoting Accountability and Ownership:

Flexibility in budgeting fosters a sense of accountability and ownership among stakeholders. When individuals and teams are involved in the budgeting process and have the flexibility to adjust their plans based on changing circumstances, they feel a greater sense of ownership over the outcomes. This promotes responsibility, innovation, and a proactive mindset, as individuals strive to achieve their financial targets while adapting to evolving conditions.

Aligning with Performance Management:

Flexible budgeting is closely linked to performance management. By incorporating variances between actual and budgeted results, organizations can assess their performance objectively and identify areas for improvement. It provides a framework for evaluating the effectiveness of financial strategies and identifying opportunities for efficiency gains. The ability to analyze and respond to variances helps organizations make data, driven decisions and continuously improve their financial performance.

Supporting Long, Term Sustainability:

A flexible budget takes into account both short, term needs and long, term sustainability. It allows organizations to balance their financial obligations and strategic objectives while considering the broader economic, social, and environmental impact of their decisions. By promoting a holistic view of financial planning, flexible budgeting supports long, term sustainability and responsible resource management.

Fixed Budget vs. Flexible Budget

Fixed Budget vs. Flexible Budget: Finding the Right Approach

Budgeting is a crucial process for individuals, businesses, and organizations to manage their finances effectively. It provides a roadmap for allocating resources, setting financial goals, and making informed decisions. Two common budgeting approaches are fixed budgeting and flexible budgeting. Below we will explore the differences between fixed budgeting and flexible budgeting, their advantages and disadvantages, and their relevance to financial management.

Understanding Fixed Budgeting:

Fixed budgeting, also known as static budgeting, is a traditional approach where financial plans are based on fixed assumptions and predetermined figures. It is created at the beginning of a period and remains unchanged, regardless of actual performance or external factors. Fixed budgeting assumes a constant level of activity and does not account for variations in revenues or costs.

Exploring Flexible Budgeting:

Flexible budgeting, on the other hand, takes into account the dynamic nature of business operations. It is designed to adapt to changes in activity levels, revenues, and costs. A flexible budget is based on different activity levels or sales volumes, allowing for adjustments to revenue and expense projections. It provides a more accurate representation of the financial situation based on the actual level of activity.

Adapting to Changing Circumstances:

One of the main differences between fixed budgeting and flexible budgeting is their adaptability to changing circumstances. Fixed budgets can become obsolete when unforeseen events occur, such as economic downturns, market fluctuations, or unexpected expenses. In contrast, flexible budgets provide organizations with the ability to adjust their financial plans in response to such changes. This adaptability enhances the organization's ability to navigate uncertainties and make informed decisions.

Managing Variability:

Fixed budgets assume a constant level of activity and often do not account for variations in revenues or costs. As a result, actual performance can deviate significantly from the budgeted figures. This can make it challenging for organizations to assess their financial performance accurately and allocate resources effectively. In contrast, flexible budgets consider different levels of activity and allow for adjustments in revenues and costs based on the actual level of activity. This enables organizations to manage variability and make more realistic financial projections.

Decision, Making and Performance Evaluation:

Fixed budgets can limit decision, making flexibility since they do not allow for adjustments based on changing circumstances. This can hinder organizations' ability to respond to market conditions, seize opportunities, or address challenges effectively. In contrast, flexible budgets provide decision, makers with valuable insights into the financial implications of different scenarios. This supports better decision, making, as managers can evaluate the financial impact of alternative courses of action and allocate resources accordingly. Furthermore, flexible budgets facilitate more accurate performance evaluation by comparing actual results with budgeted amounts at the corresponding activity level.

Accountability and Motivation:

Fixed budgets can create a culture of "meeting the budget" rather than focusing on improving performance. Since the budgeted figures are fixed, individuals may be motivated to spend up to the allocated amounts, even if more efficient alternatives are available. Flexible budgets, however, encourage accountability and efficiency by allowing individuals and teams to adjust their plans based on actual circumstances. This fosters a sense of ownership and promotes a results, oriented mindset.

Challenges and Limitations:

Implementing flexible budgeting requires more effort and data analysis compared to fixed budgeting. Organizations need to establish processes for collecting and analyzing data at different activity levels, which may require additional resources and expertise. Furthermore, the accuracy of a flexible budget depends on the availability of reliable information and the organization's ability to forecast accurately. In some cases, the complexity of the organization's operations may make it more challenging to develop and implement a flexible budget.

Chapter Two

The Components of a Flexible Budget

The Components of a Flexible Budget: Enhancing Financial Planning and Analysis

In the world of budgeting, flexibility is key to effectively managing finances and adapting to changing circumstances. A flexible budget provides organizations with a powerful tool to navigate uncertainties, make informed decisions, and improve financial planning. Below we will explore the components of a flexible budget and understand how they contribute to the overall effectiveness of financial planning and analysis.

Activity Level:

At the core of a flexible budget is the consideration of different activity levels. Activity levels may vary based on factors such as sales volume, production output, or service levels. The flexible budget takes into account these variations and allows for adjustments in revenue and expense projections accordingly. By analyzing the impact of different activity levels, organizations can better understand the financial implications of their operations and make more accurate forecasts.

Revenue Projections:

Flexible budgets incorporate flexible revenue projections that align with the activity levels being considered. Revenue projections are based on realistic assumptions about pricing, market demand, and sales volume.

By estimating revenues at different activity levels, organizations can gain insights into the revenue potential under various scenarios. This helps in evaluating the financial feasibility of business plans and setting achievable revenue targets.

Variable Costs:

Variable costs are expenses that fluctuate based on the level of activity. These costs are directly linked to the production or delivery of goods and services. In a flexible budget, variable costs are adjusted to align with the corresponding activity level. Examples of variable costs include raw materials, direct labor, and sales commissions. By analyzing variable costs in relation to activity levels, organizations can gain a better understanding of the cost drivers and make informed decisions on cost control measures.

Fixed Costs:

Fixed costs, also known as period costs, do not vary with changes in activity levels. These costs remain constant over a specific period, regardless of production or sales volume. Examples of fixed costs include rent, salaries, and insurance premiums. In a flexible budget, fixed costs remain unchanged as they are not directly influenced by activity levels. However, they are still an essential component to consider as they represent the baseline expenses that organizations must cover regardless of their level of operations.

Semi, Variable Costs:

Semi, variable costs, also known as mixed costs, contain both fixed and variable components. These costs partially vary with changes in activity levels. For example, utilities expenses may have a fixed base charge plus additional charges based on usage. In a flexible budget, semi, variable costs are adjusted based on the variable portion that varies with activity levels. Analyzing semi, variable costs in a flexible budget allows organizations to identify the fixed and variable components and understand their impact on overall expenses.

Budget Variances:

Budget variances are the differences between the actual financial performance and the budgeted amounts. Flexible budgets enable organizations to analyze and track budget variances more effectively. By comparing actual results with the corresponding budgeted amounts at the corresponding activity levels, organizations can identify areas of over or under, performance. This analysis helps in identifying the root causes of variances, taking corrective actions, and improving financial performance.

Sensitivity Analysis:

Sensitivity analysis is a technique used in flexible budgeting to assess the impact of changes in key variables on the financial outcomes. By conducting sensitivity analysis, organizations can evaluate how changes in factors such as sales volume, pricing, or cost structure affect the budgeted results. This analysis helps in understanding the potential risks and opportunities associated with different scenarios, supporting more robust decision, making and risk management.

Continuous Monitoring and Adjustment:

A flexible budget is not a static document but rather a dynamic tool that requires continuous monitoring and adjustment. Organizations need to track actual results, compare them with the budgeted amounts, and make adjustments based on changes in activity levels or market conditions.

Variable Costs

Variable Costs: Understanding their Significance in Flexible Budgeting

In the world of budgeting, understanding and managing costs is essential for effective financial planning and analysis. Among the different types of costs, variable costs play a significant role in flexible budgeting. Variable costs are expenses that fluctuate in relation to the level of activity or production. Below we will explore the concept of variable costs, their importance in flexible budgeting, and how they contribute to financial decision, making.

Defining Variable Costs:

Variable costs are expenses that change proportionally with the level of activity or production. As the volume of output increases or decreases, these costs rise or fall accordingly. Variable costs are directly tied to the resources used or consumed during the production process. Examples of variable costs include raw materials, direct labor, direct sales commissions, and packaging materials.

The Significance of Variable Costs in Flexible Budgeting:

Alignment with Activity Levels:

Flexible budgeting takes into account different levels of activity or production. By including variable costs in the budgeting process, organizations can align their cost projections with the expected level of activity. This alignment allows for more accurate and realistic cost estimates, enabling better financial planning and forecasting.

Cost, Volume, Profit Analysis:

Variable costs are essential in conducting cost, volume, profit (CVP) analysis. CVP analysis helps organizations understand the relationship between costs, volume of production or sales, and profits. By analyzing the behavior of variable costs, such as their per, unit cost or cost per transaction, organizations can evaluate the impact of different activity levels on profitability.

This analysis helps in setting pricing strategies, determining breakeven points, and making informed decisions about production or sales volume targets.

Flexibility in Cost Control:

Variable costs provide organizations with opportunities for cost control and cost optimization. Since variable costs are directly tied to the level of activity, organizations have the flexibility to adjust these costs based on changing circumstances. For example, during periods of low demand or economic downturns, organizations can reduce variable costs by scaling back production, renegotiating supplier contracts, or optimizing resource utilization. This flexibility allows for better cost management and helps organizations adapt to changing market conditions.

Incremental Analysis:

Flexible budgeting involves analyzing the financial impact of incremental changes in activity levels. Variable costs are particularly relevant in incremental analysis as they directly reflect the cost implications of changes in production or sales volume. By evaluating the incremental costs and corresponding revenues, organizations can make informed decisions about the profitability of expanding operations, introducing new products, or entering new markets.

Performance Evaluation:

Variable costs play a crucial role in evaluating performance against budgeted targets. Variance analysis compares actual costs with the budgeted amounts and identifies the reasons for any variances. By analyzing the variances in variable costs, organizations can pinpoint areas of cost overruns or cost savings. This analysis helps in evaluating operational efficiency, identifying areas for improvement, and making adjustments to future budgets.

Pricing and Profit Margin Analysis:

Variable costs are directly linked to pricing decisions and profit margins. Understanding the relationship between variable costs and pricing is crucial for setting competitive prices that cover the cost of production while ensuring profitability. By analyzing variable costs, organizations can evaluate the impact of pricing strategies on profit margins, assess the sensitivity of margins to cost changes, and make pricing decisions that maximize profitability.

Resource Allocation:

Flexible budgeting allows organizations to allocate resources effectively by considering variable costs. By understanding the cost implications of different production or service levels, organizations can allocate resources in a way that optimizes efficiency and maximizes returns. This includes allocating resources to areas where variable costs are most critical or adjusting resource allocation based on changing demand patterns.

Fixed Costs

Fixed Costs: Understanding their Role in Flexible Budgeting

When it comes to budgeting and financial planning, understanding the different types of costs is crucial. Fixed costs are one such category that plays a significant role in flexible budgeting. Below we will explore the concept of fixed costs, their importance in flexible budgeting, and how they contribute to financial decision, making.

Defining Fixed Costs:

Fixed costs are expenses that remain constant irrespective of the level of production or sales volume. They do not change with variations in activity levels. These costs are incurred regardless of whether the business is operating at full capacity or experiencing low production levels. Examples of fixed costs include rent, salaries, insurance premiums, and depreciation.

The Significance of Fixed Costs in Flexible Budgeting:

Stable Cost Projection:

Fixed costs provide a stable baseline for cost projection in flexible budgeting. By understanding and accounting for fixed costs, organizations can accurately estimate their total expenses, ensuring that critical fixed expenses are covered regardless of the level of activity. This stability allows for better financial planning and forecasting.

Breakeven Analysis:

Fixed costs play a crucial role in determining the breakeven point for a business. The breakeven point is the level of sales or production at which total revenue equals total costs, resulting in neither profit nor loss. By understanding the fixed costs, organizations can calculate the minimum level of sales or production required to cover these costs. This information is invaluable in setting sales targets, pricing strategies, and assessing the financial viability of business operations.

Cost Behavior Analysis:

Fixed costs exhibit different behavior patterns compared to variable costs. While variable costs fluctuate with changes in activity levels, fixed costs remain constant. Understanding this distinction is important for cost behavior analysis in flexible budgeting. It helps organizations identify the cost structure of their operations, determine the proportion of fixed costs to total costs, and assess the impact of cost structure on profitability and decision, making.

Flexibility in Decision, Making:

While fixed costs do not change with variations in activity levels, they can still be managed strategically. In flexible budgeting, organizations have the flexibility to make decisions that impact fixed costs. For example, they can negotiate lower rental agreements, reevaluate staffing levels, or explore cost, saving measures in areas such as insurance premiums. While these decisions may not directly impact the budget in the short term, they can lead to long, term cost savings and improved financial performance.

Cost Control and Efficiency:

Fixed costs provide organizations with an opportunity to control and optimize their expenses. By understanding the magnitude of fixed costs, organizations can focus on cost control measures that reduce these expenses. This may include streamlining operations, identifying inefficiencies, and implementing cost, saving initiatives. Managing fixed costs effectively leads to improved cost control and overall operational efficiency.

Impact on Pricing and Profitability:

Fixed costs play a critical role in pricing decisions and determining profitability. By understanding the fixed cost structure, organizations can calculate the minimum pricing required to cover these costs and generate a profit. This information helps in setting competitive prices, assessing the impact of pricing changes on profitability, and making informed pricing decisions that support long, term financial sustainability.

Evaluation of Cost Variance:

Fixed costs are also important when evaluating cost variances in flexible budgeting. By comparing actual fixed costs with the budgeted amounts, organizations can identify any deviations and investigate the reasons behind them. This analysis helps in assessing cost control measures, identifying cost overruns, and making adjustments to future budget allocations.

Semi

,

variable Costs

The Dynamic Nature of Semi, variable Costs in Flexible Budgeting

Budgeting is an essential aspect of financial management for businesses, organizations, and individuals. One crucial element in budgeting is understanding the different types of costs. Semi, variable costs, also known as mixed costs, are a unique category that combines elements of both fixed and variable costs. Below we will explore the concept of semi, variable costs, their characteristics, and their relevance in flexible budgeting.

Defining Semi, variable Costs:

Semi, variable costs are expenses that contain both fixed and variable components. These costs have a fixed portion that remains constant within a certain range of activity levels, and a variable portion that changes in relation to the level of activity. Examples of semi, variable costs include utility bills, telephone bills, maintenance costs, and commissions.

Understanding Semi, variable Costs in Flexible Budgeting:

Decomposing Costs:

Semi, variable costs pose a challenge in budgeting due to their mixed nature. Flexible budgeting helps to address this challenge by allowing organizations to break down semi, variable costs into their fixed and variable components. This decomposition provides a more accurate representation of the cost structure, enabling better cost analysis and decision, making.

Cost Prediction:

Flexible budgeting allows organizations to estimate semi, variable costs more effectively. By recognizing the fixed and variable components, organizations can project the fixed portion of semi, variable costs with greater certainty. This enables more accurate cost predictions and assists in developing a comprehensive budget that aligns with the organization's activity levels.

Performance Evaluation:

Flexible budgeting helps in evaluating the performance of semi, variable costs. By comparing actual costs with the flexible budget, organizations can assess whether the actual cost fluctuations align with the expected variations based on the activity levels. This analysis helps identify cost overruns or cost savings associated with semi, variable costs, contributing to effective performance evaluation and control.

Decision, making:

Semi, variable costs impact decision, making processes in organizations. Flexible budgeting provides insights into the behavior of semi, variable costs, allowing organizations to make informed decisions. For instance, understanding the fixed portion of semi, variable costs helps in determining the minimum cost that must be covered irrespective of activity levels. This information is crucial when evaluating investment decisions or assessing the feasibility of new projects.

Adjusting Budgets:

Flexible budgeting accommodates the changing nature of semi, variable costs. As activity levels vary, organizations can adjust their budgets accordingly by accounting for the variable portion of these costs. This flexibility allows for better financial planning and resource allocation, ensuring that the budget remains responsive to the actual level of activity.

Cost Control and Efficiency:

Flexible budgeting aids in cost control and efficiency efforts related to semi, variable costs. By recognizing the fixed and variable components, organizations can focus on controlling the variable portion through measures such as energy, saving initiatives or optimizing maintenance schedules. This targeted cost control helps in achieving cost efficiencies while maintaining the necessary fixed expenses.

Variance Analysis:

Flexible budgeting provides a framework for analyzing variances related to semi, variable costs. By comparing actual costs with the budgeted amounts, organizations can identify and investigate deviations in both the fixed and variable components. This analysis helps in understanding the drivers of cost variations, making adjustments to future budget allocations, and improving overall budget accuracy.

Chapter Three

Creating a Flexible Budget

The Art of Creating a Flexible Budget: Adapting to Changing Financial Realities

Budgeting is a crucial process that allows individuals, businesses, and organizations to effectively manage their finances and allocate resources. A flexible budget is a dynamic tool that provides the flexibility to adjust and adapt to changing financial realities. Below we will explore the process of creating a flexible budget, its benefits, and its relevance in the context of financial management.

Understanding the Concept of a Flexible Budget:

A flexible budget is a budgeting approach that adjusts expenses and revenue projections based on changes in activity levels or other external factors. Unlike a traditional fixed budget, which is based on static assumptions, a flexible budget allows for variations and provides a more realistic financial plan that can adapt to fluctuations in income and expenses.

The Process of Creating a Flexible Budget:

Establish a Baseline:

The first step in creating a flexible budget is to establish a baseline. This involves identifying and documenting the current financial situation, including income sources, fixed expenses, and variable expenses. This baseline serves as the starting point for the budgeting process.

Identify Key Variables:

Next, it is important to identify the key variables that affect the budget. These variables could include factors such as sales volume, production levels, market conditions, or any other factors that impact revenue and expenses. By understanding these variables, you can create a budget that is sensitive to changes in these factors.

Determine Fixed and Variable Costs:

To create a flexible budget, it is essential to distinguish between fixed and variable costs. Fixed costs are those that remain constant regardless of changes in activity levels, such as rent or insurance. Variable costs, on the other hand, fluctuate with changes in activity levels, such as raw material costs or marketing expenses. Categorizing costs in this way helps in developing a more accurate and adaptable budget.

Set Realistic Targets:

Once fixed and variable costs are identified, it is important to set realistic targets for each category. This involves analyzing historical data, market trends, and future projections to estimate income and expenses. The targets should reflect the anticipated changes in activity levels and other relevant factors.

Create Scenarios:

A key aspect of a flexible budget is the ability to create different scenarios. These scenarios represent different potential outcomes based on varying assumptions. By creating multiple scenarios, you can assess the impact of different factors on your budget and make informed decisions.

Monitor and Adjust:

Creating a flexible budget is not a one, time task. It requires continuous monitoring and adjustment. Regularly review your budget and compare it to actual performance. Identify any deviations or discrepancies and make necessary adjustments to keep the budget aligned with your financial goals and changing circumstances.

The Benefits of a Flexible Budget:

Adaptability:

One of the primary benefits of a flexible budget is its adaptability. It allows you to respond to unexpected changes in income or expenses by adjusting your budget accordingly. This adaptability helps in maintaining financial stability and avoiding financial crises.

Accurate Financial Planning:

A flexible budget provides a more accurate representation of your financial situation. By considering variables and adjusting projections, you can make more informed decisions about resource allocation, investment opportunities, and savings targets. This accuracy enhances financial planning and decision, making.

Improved Financial Control:

With a flexible budget, you have better control over your finances. By monitoring actual performance against the budget, you can identify areas of overspending or underspending. This knowledge enables you to take corrective actions and make informed choices to optimize your financial resources.

Enhanced Decision, making:

A flexible budget allows you to evaluate the financial impact of different scenarios and make better, informed decisions. You can assess the potential outcomes of different strategies, investments, or cost, saving initiatives. This enhanced decision, making capability contributes to long, term financial success.

Step

,

by

,

Step Guide to Building a Flexible Budget

Building a Flexible Budget: A Step, by, Step Guide to Financial Adaptability

Budgeting is a fundamental tool for effective financial management. It allows individuals, businesses, and organizations to plan their income and expenses, allocate resources, and achieve their financial goals. A flexible budget takes this process one step further by incorporating adaptability and responsiveness to changing circumstances. Below we will provide a step, by, step guide to building a flexible budget, exploring its benefits, and its importance in achieving financial success.

Step 1: Establish Your Financial Goals and Objectives

Before diving into budgeting, it's crucial to identify your financial goals and objectives. These could include saving for retirement, paying off debts, investing in education, or purchasing a new home. Understanding your priorities will shape the direction and focus of your budget.

Step 2: Gather Financial Data and Income Information

To build an effective flexible budget, you need a clear picture of your current financial situation. Gather all relevant financial data, including bank statements, pay stubs, bills, and any other financial documents. This will help you determine your income sources, fixed expenses, and variable expenses.

Step 3: Identify Fixed and Variable Expenses

Differentiating between fixed and variable expenses is a crucial step in building a flexible budget. Fixed expenses, such as rent or mortgage payments, insurance premiums, and loan repayments, remain constant regardless of changes in income or activity levels. Variable expenses, on the other hand, fluctuate based on factors like discretionary spending, utilities, or entertainment.

Step 4: Analyze Historical Data and Identify Patterns

Review your past financial records and analyze your spending patterns. Look for trends, seasonal variations, or any irregularities in your income and expenses. This analysis will help you identify areas where you can potentially adjust your budget based on previous patterns and behaviors.

Step 5: Estimate Variable Expenses Based on Activity Levels

Since variable expenses fluctuate with activity levels, estimate these expenses based on your expected level of activity. For example, if you are planning a vacation or foresee higher utility costs during the summer months, adjust your budget accordingly. Consider factors such as upcoming events, holidays, or changes in lifestyle that may impact your expenses.

Step 6: Consider Multiple Scenarios

One of the key features of a flexible budget is its ability to accommodate different scenarios. Consider various scenarios that may impact your income and expenses. For example, simulate scenarios like a decrease in income, unexpected expenses, or changes in market conditions. By doing so, you can anticipate potential challenges and prepare accordingly.

Step 7: Set Realistic Targets and Allocate Resources

Based on your financial goals, historical data, and estimated expenses, set realistic targets for each budget category. Allocate resources accordingly to ensure that your income covers your expenses while leaving room for savings and investments. Be mindful of balancing your needs, wants, and long, term financial objectives.

Step 8: Monitor and Review Regularly

Building a flexible budget is an ongoing process. Monitor your actual income and expenses regularly and compare them to your budgeted amounts. Identify any discrepancies or deviations and make necessary adjustments. Regular reviews will enable you to stay on track and ensure that your budget remains aligned with your financial goals.

Step 9: Embrace Change and Adaptability

Flexibility is at the core of a flexible budget. Embrace change and be open to adjusting your budget as circumstances evolve. Life is dynamic, and unexpected events can arise. By maintaining a flexible mindset, you can adapt your budget to accommodate unforeseen circumstances while staying focused on your financial objectives.

Step 10: Seek Professional Advice if Needed

If you feel overwhelmed or require expert guidance, don't hesitate to seek the assistance of a financial advisor.

Budgeting for Different Levels of Activity

Adapting Budgeting for Different Levels of Activity: A Dynamic Approach to Financial Management

Budgeting is an essential tool for managing finances effectively. It provides a framework for planning and allocating resources based on projected income and expenses. However, traditional budgeting models often fail to account for changes in activity levels, resulting in inflexible budgets that may not accurately reflect financial realities. Below we will explore the concept of budgeting for different levels of activity and its relationship to flexible budgeting, discussing its importance and benefits in achieving financial success.

Understanding Budgeting for Different Levels of Activity:

Budgeting for different levels of activity refers to the process of adjusting income and expenses based on the varying volume of business activity or other factors that impact financial outcomes. It recognizes that revenue and costs are not static but vary depending on factors such as sales volume, production levels, market conditions, or customer demand. By incorporating this dynamic element into budgeting, organizations can create budgets that are more responsive to changes in activity levels and provide a more accurate financial plan.

Importance of Budgeting for Different Levels of Activity:

Realistic Financial Planning:

Budgeting for different levels of activity allows organizations to develop more realistic financial plans. By considering the impact of changes in activity levels, such as seasonal variations or fluctuations in demand, budgets can better align with actual revenue and expenses. This enhances the organization's ability to set achievable financial targets and make informed decisions.

Resource Allocation:

Budgeting for different levels of activity enables organizations to allocate resources efficiently. When activity levels are high, businesses can allocate more resources to meet increased demand, expand operations, or invest in growth opportunities. Conversely, during periods of low activity, resources can be allocated more conservatively, allowing for cost control and preservation of capital.

Cost Management:

Different levels of activity often correspond to varying costs. For example, production costs may increase with higher output, or sales and marketing expenses may rise during peak periods. By factoring in these variable costs, organizations can better manage and control their expenses, ensuring that costs are proportionate to revenue and optimizing overall profitability.

Accurate Financial Forecasting:

Budgeting for different levels of activity enhances financial forecasting accuracy. By considering the impact of activity fluctuations, organizations can forecast revenue and expenses more effectively. This allows for better anticipation of cash flow, identification of potential gaps or surpluses, and proactive planning to address financial needs.

Performance Evaluation:

Budgeting for different levels of activity enables organizations to assess performance more accurately. By comparing actual financial results to the corresponding activity level, organizations can evaluate their efficiency and effectiveness. This assessment helps identify areas of improvement, optimize resource utilization, and align performance metrics with specific activity levels.

Benefits of Budgeting for Different Levels of Activity:

Flexibility and Adaptability:

Budgeting for different levels of activity provides greater flexibility and adaptability. It allows organizations to adjust their budgets in response to changing circumstances, ensuring that financial plans remain relevant and realistic. This flexibility enables businesses to seize opportunities, navigate challenges, and optimize resource allocation at any given activity level.

Improved Decision, making:

By incorporating activity, based budgeting, organizations can make more informed decisions. Managers have access to accurate financial data that reflects the specific activity level, enabling them to evaluate the financial impact of different courses of action. This improves decision, making, promotes strategic planning, and supports long, term business success.

Enhanced Communication and Accountability:

Budgeting for different levels of activity promotes communication and accountability within an organization. With budgets that align with specific activity levels, team members have a clearer understanding of their roles and responsibilities. This clarity fosters better collaboration, enhances performance accountability, and supports a shared understanding of financial objectives.

Estimating Costs Accurately

Estimating Costs Accurately: The Key to Effective Budgeting and Flexible Financial Planning

Accurate cost estimation is a critical component of effective budgeting and financial planning. Whether it's for personal finances, business operations, or project management, estimating costs with precision is essential for making informed decisions and achieving financial goals. Below we will explore the importance of estimating costs accurately in relation to flexible budgeting, discussing the challenges involved, and providing strategies for improving cost estimation practices.

The Significance of Accurate Cost Estimation:

Accurate cost estimation is vital for several reasons:

Budgeting and Financial Planning:

Cost estimation forms the foundation of budgeting and financial planning processes. It allows individuals and organizations to allocate resources effectively, set realistic financial targets, and monitor financial performance. Accurate cost estimation ensures that budgets are based on reliable information, enabling better decision, making and reducing the risk of financial shortfalls.

Decision, Making:

Accurate cost estimation provides essential insights for decision, making. It helps individuals and organizations evaluate the financial feasibility of projects, investments, and initiatives. By understanding the expected costs, stakeholders can assess the potential return on investment and make informed choices about resource allocation and prioritization.

Risk Management:

Accurate cost estimation plays a crucial role in managing financial risks. Overestimating costs may result in unnecessary expenditures and reduced profitability, while underestimating costs can lead to budget overruns and financial difficulties. Accurate cost estimation helps mitigate these risks by providing a realistic assessment of potential expenses and allowing for contingency planning.

Challenges in Cost Estimation:

Accurate cost estimation is not without its challenges. Some common obstacles include:

Lack of Historical Data:

Estimating costs accurately can be challenging, particularly when historical data is limited or unavailable. Without a reliable reference point, it becomes more difficult to assess the expected costs based on past performance. In such cases, alternative methods, such as benchmarking or industry research, may be necessary to derive reasonable cost estimates.

Complexity and Interdependencies:

In many situations, costs are interdependent and influenced by various factors. For instance, in a construction project, costs for materials, labor, and equipment are interconnected. Changes in one aspect can impact the overall cost structure. Understanding and accounting for these interdependencies is crucial for accurate cost estimation.

Uncertainties and Variables:

The future is inherently uncertain, and cost estimation involves predicting future expenses. Factors such as market conditions, regulatory changes, or unforeseen events can introduce uncertainties that make accurate estimation challenging. It is important to consider these variables and incorporate a degree of flexibility into the cost estimation process.

Strategies for Improving Cost Estimation:

While cost estimation may present challenges, several strategies can help improve accuracy:

Gather Sufficient Information:

To estimate costs accurately, gather as much relevant information as possible. Consult historical data, industry benchmarks, and expert opinions to inform your estimation process. Additionally, consider the specific details of the project or context to account for unique factors that may impact costs.

Break Down Costs:

Breaking down costs into their components can enhance accuracy. Identify and categorize different cost elements, such as materials, labor, equipment, and overheads. This granular approach allows for a more detailed assessment of each aspect, leading to a more precise estimation.

Utilize Multiple Estimation Techniques:

Don't rely solely on one estimation technique. Instead, use a combination of approaches to triangulate and validate the results. Common estimation techniques include top, down estimation, bottom, up estimation, analogous estimation (based on similar past projects), and parametric estimation (using mathematical models and variables).

Involve Stakeholders and Experts:

Engaging stakeholders and experts in the estimation process can provide valuable insights and diverse perspectives.

Chapter Four

Flexible Budget Variances

Understanding Flexible Budget Variances: Unveiling Insights for Financial Analysis and Decision, Making

Flexible budget variances are a powerful tool for analyzing financial performance and assessing the effectiveness of flexible budgeting. By comparing actual results with the flexible budget, organizations can gain valuable insights into their revenue generation and cost management. Below we will explore the concept of flexible budget variances, their significance in the context of flexible budgeting, and how they contribute to informed financial analysis and decision, making.

The Concept of Flexible Budget Variances:

Flexible budget variances are the differences between actual results and the amounts projected in the flexible budget. While a traditional fixed budget is based on static assumptions, a flexible budget adjusts the budgeted amounts based on changes in activity levels. Therefore, variances arise due to deviations between actual activity levels and the flexible budget's assumptions.

Types of Flexible Budget Variances:

Flexible budget variances can be classified into two main types:

Revenue Variances:

Revenue variances measure the difference between actual revenue and the revenue projected in the flexible budget. A favorable revenue variance indicates that actual revenue exceeds the flexible budget, while an unfavorable variance suggests that actual revenue falls short of the flexible budget.

Expense Variances:

Expense variances reflect the differences between actual expenses and the expenses estimated in the flexible budget. A favorable expense variance occurs when actual expenses are lower than the flexible budget, indicating cost savings. Conversely, an unfavorable expense variance arises when actual expenses exceed the flexible budget, signaling cost overruns.

Interpreting Flexible Budget Variances:

Interpreting flexible budget variances involves analyzing the causes and implications of the variances. By understanding the underlying reasons for the variances, organizations can identify areas of strength or weakness and take appropriate actions. Some key considerations include:

Activity Level Variances:

Activity level variances occur when the actual level of activity deviates from the assumed activity level in the flexible budget. These variances directly impact both revenue and expenses. A favorable activity level variance indicates higher activity levels than anticipated, while an unfavorable variance suggests lower activity levels.

Price Variances:

Price variances arise due to differences in prices or rates from those assumed in the flexible budget. For revenue, a favorable price variance may indicate higher prices or increased sales volume, while an unfavorable variance may reflect lower prices or decreased sales volume. For expenses, a favorable price variance indicates cost savings, while an unfavorable variance represents cost increases.

Efficiency Variances:

Efficiency variances measure the effectiveness and efficiency of resource utilization. They reflect differences in the actual quantity of resources used compared to the quantity assumed in the flexible budget. A favorable efficiency variance implies efficient resource usage, while an unfavorable variance suggests inefficiencies.

Significance of Material Variances:

Not all variances are created equal. It is crucial to focus on material variances that have a significant impact on financial performance. By prioritizing material variances, organizations can allocate their resources and attention where it matters most, enabling more effective financial management.

Benefits of Analyzing Flexible Budget Variances:

Performance Evaluation:

Flexible budget variances serve as a tool for evaluating performance against targets. They highlight areas of success and areas that require improvement. By analyzing the variances, organizations can gain a comprehensive understanding of their financial performance and take appropriate corrective actions.

Identifying Operational Efficiencies:

Flexible budget variances offer insights into operational efficiencies. Favorable variances can indicate effective cost management practices, streamlined processes, or successful revenue generation strategies. Understanding these efficiencies allows organizations to replicate successful practices and implement cost, saving measures.

Understanding Variances

Unveiling Insights: Understanding Variances and Their Role in Financial Analysis

Variances play a crucial role in financial analysis by highlighting differences between planned and actual outcomes. They provide valuable insights into the performance of individuals, businesses, and organizations, allowing for informed decision, making and continuous improvement. Below we will explore the concept of variances, their significance in financial analysis, and their relationship to flexible budgeting.

What Are Variances?

Variances refer to the differences between planned or budgeted amounts and actual results. They can arise in various areas, including revenue, expenses, production costs, or performance metrics. Variances can be favorable (positive) or unfavorable (negative) depending on whether actual results exceed or fall short of the planned amounts.

Types of Variances:

Revenue Variances:

Revenue variances measure the difference between the actual revenue and the budgeted or expected revenue. A favorable revenue variance indicates that actual revenue exceeded the budgeted amount, while an unfavorable variance suggests that actual revenue fell short of the budgeted amount. Revenue variances can provide insights into the effectiveness of sales strategies, market conditions, or customer demand.

Expense Variances:

Expense variances compare actual expenses with the budgeted or expected expenses. A favorable expense variance occurs when actual expenses are lower than the budgeted amount, indicating cost savings. Conversely, an unfavorable expense variance arises when actual expenses exceed the budgeted amount, signaling potential inefficiencies or unexpected costs.

Production Cost Variances:

Production cost variances are commonly used in manufacturing or production, oriented industries. They compare actual production costs with the standard or budgeted costs. Favorable production cost variances indicate cost savings resulting from efficient operations, while unfavorable variances suggest cost overruns or inefficiencies.

Performance Metric Variances:

Performance metric variances assess the difference between actual performance and the planned or target performance. These variances can include metrics such as sales volume, customer satisfaction ratings, or productivity measures. Analyzing performance metric variances allows organizations to identify areas for improvement and align their efforts with strategic objectives.

Significance of Variances in Financial Analysis:

Performance Evaluation:

Variances are an essential tool for evaluating performance. By comparing actual results with the planned amounts, variances provide a quantitative assessment of performance. They highlight areas of success or underperformance, enabling organizations to identify strengths and weaknesses and make informed decisions.

Identifying Trends and Patterns:

Analyzing variances over time helps identify trends and patterns in financial performance. By examining the consistency and magnitude of variances, organizations can gain insights into recurring issues, seasonal fluctuations, or changing market dynamics. This information aids in strategic planning and resource allocation.

Cost Control and Efficiency:

Expense variances, in particular, offer insights into cost control and efficiency. Favorable expense variances indicate effective cost management practices, efficient resource allocation, or successful cost, saving initiatives. Organizations can leverage this information to identify best practices and implement measures that optimize cost efficiency.

Decision, Making and Planning:

Variances contribute to informed decision, making and planning. By understanding the reasons behind variances, organizations can identify the factors driving positive outcomes and replicate successful strategies. Conversely, unfavorable variances provide opportunities to investigate the root causes, develop corrective actions, and improve future performance.

Flexible Budgeting and Variances:

Flexible budgeting plays a significant role in understanding and analyzing variances. Unlike fixed budgets that are static, flexible budgets adjust to changes in activity levels or other external factors. This flexibility allows for more accurate budgeting and variance analysis, as the budgeted amounts are aligned with the actual level of activity.

Analyzing Variances in a Flexible Budget

Unraveling Insights: Analyzing Variances in a Flexible Budget

Analyzing variances is a crucial aspect of financial management, enabling organizations to assess their performance and make informed decisions. When combined with a flexible budget, variance analysis becomes even more powerful, providing deeper insights into the factors influencing financial outcomes. Below we will explore the process of analyzing variances in a flexible budget, highlighting its significance in financial analysis and its relationship to flexible budgeting.

Understanding Variances in a Flexible Budget:

A flexible budget is a dynamic financial tool that adjusts revenue and expense projections based on changes in activity levels. It provides a more accurate representation of expected financial outcomes compared to a fixed budget, which remains static regardless of fluctuations in activity. Variances in a flexible budget arise from deviations between actual results and the amounts projected in the flexible budget. Analyzing these variances helps identify the reasons behind the discrepancies and allows for better understanding of financial performance.

The Process of Analyzing Variances:

Identify Variances:

The first step in analyzing variances in a flexible budget is to identify the discrepancies between the actual results and the flexible budget amounts. This involves comparing the actual revenue and expenses with the corresponding budgeted amounts. By calculating the difference, organizations can determine the magnitude and direction of each variance.

Categorize Variances:

Once the variances are identified, they can be categorized into revenue variances and expense variances. Revenue variances represent the difference between actual revenue and the revenue projected in the flexible budget.

Expense variances, on the other hand, reflect the difference between actual expenses and the expenses estimated in the flexible budget.

Assess Favorable and Unfavorable Variances:

After categorizing the variances, it is important to assess whether each variance is favorable or unfavorable. A favorable variance occurs when the actual result exceeds the budgeted amount, indicating better, than, expected performance. Conversely, an unfavorable variance indicates that the actual result falls short of the budgeted amount.

Determine the Causes:

To understand the reasons behind the variances, it is crucial to investigate and determine their causes. This may involve analyzing the underlying factors that contributed to the variances. For example, revenue variances may be influenced by changes in pricing, sales volume, or market conditions, while expense variances may be driven by fluctuations in costs or changes in production levels.

Evaluate the Significance:

Not all variances carry the same level of significance. It is important to evaluate the materiality of each variance, considering its impact on overall financial performance. Material variances with substantial effects should be prioritized for further analysis and action.

Take Corrective Actions:

Based on the causes identified and the significance of the variances, organizations can take appropriate corrective actions. This may involve adjusting strategies, refining operations, implementing cost, saving measures, or capitalizing on opportunities highlighted by favorable variances. The goal is to align future actions with the desired financial objectives.

The Significance of Analyzing Variances in a Flexible Budget:

Performance Evaluation:

Analyzing variances in a flexible budget enables a comprehensive evaluation of financial performance. It provides a deeper understanding of how well the organization has performed compared to the budgeted expectations. By identifying areas of over, performance or under, performance, organizations can make informed decisions to improve their financial outcomes.

Continuous Improvement:

Variance analysis supports a culture of continuous improvement within an organization. By examining the causes of variances, organizations can identify areas where processes can be refined, efficiencies can be enhanced, or performance can be optimized. This continuous improvement approach fosters ongoing financial success.

Using Variances for Decision Making

Harnessing Variances: Using Variances for Informed Decision Making

Variances play a crucial role in financial analysis, providing insights into the performance of organizations and individuals. By comparing actual results with planned or budgeted amounts, variances highlight areas of strength, weaknesses, and opportunities for improvement. In the context of flexible budgeting, analyzing variances becomes even more valuable, as it enables informed decision, making based on real, time financial data. Below we will explore how variances can be used for decision, making and their relevance to flexible budgeting.

Understanding Variances:

Variances represent the differences between actual results and the planned or budgeted amounts. They can arise in various aspects, such as revenue, expenses, production costs, or performance metrics. Variances can be favorable (positive) or unfavorable (negative), depending on whether actual results exceed or fall short of the planned amounts.

Using Variances for Decision, Making:

Identifying Performance Deviations:

Variances act as red flags, drawing attention to areas where actual performance deviates from the planned or expected outcomes. By analyzing variances, organizations can identify which areas are performing well and which require attention. This knowledge aids decision, making by highlighting where resources and efforts should be directed.

Diagnosing Root Causes:

Variances provide insights into the underlying causes of performance deviations. Organizations can use variance analysis to investigate the factors influencing the variances and identify the root causes. For example, a revenue variance may indicate changes in market conditions, pricing strategies, or customer behavior, while an expense variance may be attributed to cost overruns, inefficient processes, or unexpected events. Understanding these causes is essential for making informed decisions.

Assessing Financial Impact:

Variances help quantify the financial impact of performance deviations. By comparing the actual results with the planned amounts, organizations can determine the magnitude of the variances and assess their implications. This information allows decision, makers to evaluate the financial consequences of different courses of action and prioritize areas that require immediate attention.

Prioritizing Resource Allocation:

Variances assist in prioritizing resource allocation. Favorable variances indicate areas of strength where resources can be allocated more efficiently or redirected to other strategic initiatives. Unfavorable variances, on the other hand, signal areas that require corrective actions or additional resources to bring performance back in line with expectations. By aligning resource allocation with the identified variances, organizations can optimize their financial outcomes.

Informing Strategic Planning:

Variances provide valuable information for strategic planning. They reveal trends and patterns in financial performance, highlighting areas of success and areas that require improvement. By analyzing variances over time, organizations can identify opportunities for growth, operational efficiencies, or cost, saving measures. This information informs the development of strategic plans and allows for the alignment of financial goals with broader organizational objectives.

Setting Realistic Budgets:

Variances play a critical role in setting realistic budgets. By analyzing variances from previous periods, organizations can gain insights into the accuracy of their budgeting process. This information can be used to refine budgeting assumptions, estimate revenues and expenses more accurately, and ensure that future budgets are realistic and achievable.

Facilitating Continuous Improvement:

Variance analysis supports a culture of continuous improvement within organizations. By identifying performance deviations and their causes, organizations can implement corrective actions and monitor their effectiveness. Regular variance analysis promotes learning, adaptability, and the implementation of best practices to drive ongoing improvements in financial performance.

Relevance of Variances to Flexible Budgeting:

Flexible budgeting enhances the significance of variances in decision, making. Traditional fixed budgets often fail to account for changes in activity levels or other external factors. In contrast, flexible budgets adjust the budgeted amounts based on these changes, providing a more accurate reflection of expected financial outcomes.

Chapter Five

Flexible Budgets and Performance Evaluation

Unleashing Performance Insights: Flexible Budgets and their Role in Performance Evaluation

Performance evaluation is a critical aspect of organizational success, allowing for the assessment of financial performance and the identification of areas for improvement. In the realm of financial management, flexible budgets play a pivotal role in performance evaluation. By providing a dynamic framework that adjusts to changes in activity levels, flexible budgets enable organizations to evaluate their performance accurately. Below we will explore the relationship between flexible budgets and performance evaluation, emphasizing the benefits and relevance of flexible budgeting in assessing financial outcomes.

Understanding Flexible Budgets:

Flexible budgets are dynamic financial tools that adjust revenue and expense projections based on changes in activity levels. Unlike fixed budgets, which are based on static assumptions, flexible budgets take into account the fluctuating nature of business operations. This flexibility enables organizations to evaluate their financial performance more accurately and make informed decisions.

The Role of Flexible Budgets in Performance Evaluation:

Accurate Performance Measurement:

Flexible budgets facilitate accurate performance measurement by providing a benchmark that aligns with the actual level of activity. They enable organizations to evaluate their financial results based on the specific activity levels achieved during the evaluation period. By comparing actual performance against the flexible budget, organizations gain a clearer understanding of their achievements, strengths, and areas for improvement.

Variance Analysis:

Flexible budgets facilitate in, depth variance analysis, which is a vital component of performance evaluation. By comparing actual results with the flexible budget, organizations can identify and analyze variances, which are the differences between the two. Variance analysis helps pinpoint the reasons behind the discrepancies, such as changes in activity levels, pricing, costs, or external factors. This analysis provides valuable insights for decision, making and improving future performance.

Evaluating Cost Control and Efficiency:

Flexible budgets enable organizations to evaluate cost control and efficiency. By comparing actual expenses with the corresponding budgeted amounts, organizations can assess how effectively resources have been utilized. Favorable variances indicate cost savings and efficient resource allocation, while unfavorable variances may highlight inefficiencies or unexpected cost overruns. This evaluation helps organizations identify areas for improvement and implement cost, saving measures.

Assessing Revenue Generation:

Flexible budgets allow organizations to evaluate their revenue generation efforts accurately. By comparing actual revenue with the revenue projected in the flexible budget, organizations can assess their sales performance and revenue, generating strategies. Favorable revenue variances indicate successful sales initiatives, increased market share, or higher customer demand. Unfavorable revenue variances may prompt a reassessment of pricing strategies, marketing efforts, or customer retention tactics.

Strategic Planning and Decision, Making:

Flexible budgets support strategic planning and decision, making by providing timely and relevant financial information. Performance evaluation based on flexible budgets helps identify trends, patterns, and potential opportunities. Organizations can use this information to make informed decisions regarding resource allocation, investment priorities, cost management strategies, and operational improvements. The insights gained from performance evaluation contribute to the formulation of effective strategies that align with organizational objectives.

Benefits of Using Flexible Budgets for Performance Evaluation:

Enhanced Accuracy:

Flexible budgets enhance the accuracy of performance evaluation by accounting for changes in activity levels. Unlike fixed budgets, which may become obsolete in dynamic business environments, flexible budgets provide a more realistic reflection of actual performance. This accuracy helps organizations identify their true financial achievements and areas requiring attention.

Better Accountability:

Flexible budgets improve accountability by aligning performance evaluation with the specific activity levels achieved. By evaluating performance based on activity, specific benchmarks, organizations can hold individuals or departments accountable for their contributions to financial outcomes. This accountability fosters a sense of responsibility and encourages individuals to strive for improved performance.

Role of a Flexible Budget in Performance Measurement

Unveiling Performance Insights: The Role of a Flexible Budget in Performance Measurement

Performance measurement is a crucial aspect of assessing organizational success and identifying areas for improvement. In the realm of financial management, a flexible budget plays a pivotal role in accurately measuring performance. By adjusting to changes in activity levels, a flexible budget provides a dynamic framework for performance evaluation. Below we will explore the significance of a flexible budget in performance measurement, emphasizing its benefits and relevance to achieving organizational objectives.

Understanding the Flexible Budget:

A flexible budget is a financial tool that adjusts revenue and expense projections based on changes in activity levels. Unlike a fixed budget, which remains static regardless of actual activity, a flexible budget provides a more accurate reflection of expected financial outcomes. It aligns with the specific activity levels achieved during the performance evaluation period.

The Role of a Flexible Budget in Performance Measurement:

Accurate Performance Evaluation:

A flexible budget enables accurate performance evaluation by considering the actual activity levels achieved. It provides a benchmark that aligns with the level of activity during the performance evaluation period. By comparing actual performance against the flexible budget, organizations can assess their achievements, strengths, and areas for improvement more accurately. This accuracy enhances the effectiveness of performance measurement.

Comprehensive Variance Analysis:

Variance analysis is a critical component of performance measurement, and a flexible budget facilitates in, depth variance analysis. By comparing actual results with the flexible budget, organizations can identify and analyze variances—the differences between the two. Variances may arise due to changes in activity levels, pricing, costs, or external factors. Through variance analysis, organizations gain valuable insights into the drivers behind the discrepancies, enabling them to make informed decisions and take corrective actions.

Identifying Strengths and Weaknesses:

A flexible budget allows organizations to identify their strengths and weaknesses more effectively. By comparing actual performance with the flexible budget, organizations can pinpoint areas where they have outperformed expectations (favorable variances) and areas that require improvement (unfavorable variances). This identification helps organizations focus their efforts on leveraging their strengths and addressing their weaknesses to enhance overall performance.

Evaluation of Cost Control and Efficiency:

A flexible budget facilitates the evaluation of cost control and efficiency. By comparing actual expenses with the corresponding budgeted amounts in the flexible budget, organizations can assess how effectively resources have been utilized. Favorable variances indicate cost savings and efficient resource allocation, while unfavorable variances may highlight inefficiencies or unexpected cost overruns. This evaluation enables organizations to identify areas for improvement and implement cost, saving measures, thus enhancing cost control and efficiency.

Assessment of Revenue Generation:

The flexible budget allows organizations to assess their revenue generation efforts accurately. By comparing actual revenue with the revenue projected in the flexible budget, organizations can evaluate their sales performance and revenue, generating strategies. Favorable revenue variances indicate successful sales initiatives, increased market share, or higher customer demand. Unfavorable revenue variances prompt organizations to reassess pricing strategies, marketing efforts, or customer retention tactics. This assessment facilitates better revenue management and drives strategic decision, making.

Alignment with Strategic Objectives:

A flexible budget plays a pivotal role in aligning performance measurement with strategic objectives. By adjusting the budgeted amounts based on changes in activity levels, a flexible budget reflects the dynamic nature of the business environment. This alignment ensures that performance measurement focuses on the key activities and targets outlined in the organization's strategic plan. By evaluating performance against the flexible budget, organizations can gauge their progress toward strategic objectives and make informed adjustments to their strategies if necessary.

Advantages of Using Flexible Budgets for Performance Evaluation

Embracing Flexibility: The Advantages of Using Flexible Budgets for Performance Evaluation

Performance evaluation is a critical process that enables organizations to assess their financial performance, identify areas of improvement, and make informed decisions. In this regard, flexible budgets offer a valuable tool for performance evaluation. Unlike static budgets, flexible budgets adjust to changes in activity levels, providing a more accurate assessment of performance. Below we will explore the advantages of using flexible budgets for performance evaluation, highlighting their benefits and relevance in achieving organizational objectives.

Accurate Performance Measurement:

One of the key advantages of using flexible budgets for performance evaluation is the accuracy it provides. Unlike static budgets that may become irrelevant in dynamic business environments, flexible budgets align with the specific activity levels achieved during the evaluation period. This alignment ensures that the performance evaluation reflects the actual performance, providing a more accurate assessment of achievements and areas for improvement.

Improved Variance Analysis:

Flexible budgets enable organizations to conduct more insightful variance analysis. By comparing actual results with the flexible budget, organizations can identify and analyze variances—the differences between the two. Variances may arise due to changes in activity levels, pricing, costs, or external factors. The flexibility of the budget allows for a more detailed examination of these variances, leading to a deeper understanding of their causes and implications. This enhanced variance analysis facilitates informed decision, making and targeted actions to address performance gaps.

Enhanced Cost Control and Efficiency:

Flexible budgets play a crucial role in evaluating cost control and efficiency. By comparing actual expenses with the corresponding budgeted amounts in the flexible budget, organizations can assess how effectively resources have been utilized. Favorable variances indicate cost savings and efficient resource allocation, while unfavorable variances may highlight inefficiencies or unexpected cost overruns. This evaluation allows organizations to identify areas for improvement, implement cost, saving measures, and optimize resource allocation, leading to improved cost control and operational efficiency.

Accurate Revenue Assessment:

Flexible budgets enable organizations to accurately assess their revenue generation efforts. By comparing actual revenue with the revenue projected in the flexible budget, organizations can evaluate their sales performance and revenue, generating strategies. Favorable revenue variances indicate successful sales initiatives, increased market share, or higher customer demand. Unfavorable revenue variances prompt organizations to reassess pricing strategies, marketing efforts, or customer retention tactics. This accurate revenue assessment helps organizations refine their revenue management strategies, identify growth opportunities, and align their efforts with market dynamics.

Strategic Decision, Making:

Flexible budgets support strategic decision, making by providing timely and accurate financial information. Performance evaluation based on flexible budgets helps identify trends, patterns, and potential opportunities. Organizations can use this information to make informed decisions regarding resource allocation, investment priorities, cost management strategies, and operational improvements. The insights gained from performance evaluation based on flexible budgets contribute to the formulation of effective strategies that align with organizational objectives.

Adaptability to Changing Circumstances:

Flexible budgets offer the advantage of adaptability to changing circumstances. In a dynamic business environment, activity levels, market conditions, and external factors can fluctuate. Traditional fixed budgets may fail to capture these changes, leading to inaccurate performance evaluation. However, flexible budgets adjust to these fluctuations, ensuring that performance measurement remains relevant and reflective of the prevailing conditions. This adaptability allows organizations to navigate uncertainties, seize opportunities, and make agile decisions.

Motivation and Accountability:

Using flexible budgets for performance evaluation can enhance motivation and accountability within the organization. By aligning the budgeted amounts with the actual level of activity, employees can clearly understand their performance expectations. This clarity fosters a sense of ownership and accountability, as employees strive to meet or exceed the budgeted targets. The alignment of performance evaluation with flexible budgets promotes transparency, enhances motivation, and supports a culture of continuous improvement.

Potential Pitfalls and Solutions

Navigating the Path: Potential Pitfalls and Solutions in Flexible Budgeting

Flexible budgeting is a powerful financial management tool that allows organizations to adapt to changing circumstances and make informed decisions. However, like any methodology, flexible budgeting is not without its potential pitfalls. Recognizing these pitfalls and implementing appropriate solutions is crucial to ensure the effectiveness of flexible budgeting. Below we will explore some common pitfalls associated with flexible budgeting and propose solutions to overcome them, enabling organizations to harness the full potential of this approach.

Pitfall 1: Inaccurate Activity Level Assumptions

One of the key challenges in flexible budgeting is accurately estimating the activity levels that drive the budget. Inaccurate assumptions about the level of activity can lead to distorted budgeted amounts and ineffective performance evaluation.

Solution: To address this pitfall, organizations should invest time and effort in gathering reliable data and conducting thorough analysis. Historical data, market research, industry benchmarks, and input from relevant stakeholders can provide valuable insights for accurate activity level assumptions. Regularly reviewing and updating these assumptions based on current market conditions and organizational objectives will enhance the accuracy of the flexible budget.

Pitfall 2: Insufficient Communication and Stakeholder Engagement

Lack of effective communication and stakeholder engagement can undermine the success of flexible budgeting. When key stakeholders are not involved or informed about the flexible budgeting process, they may have limited understanding of the underlying assumptions and may not fully align their actions and decisions with the budgeted targets.

Solution: Organizations should prioritize communication and stakeholder engagement throughout the flexible budgeting process. This includes clearly communicating the objectives, assumptions, and expectations of the flexible budget to all relevant stakeholders. Regularly engaging with stakeholders through meetings, workshops, and feedback sessions fosters a sense of ownership and promotes alignment between individual and organizational goals.

Pitfall 3: Failure to Monitor and Analyze Variances

Variances, the differences between actual results and the flexible budget, provide valuable insights for performance evaluation and decision, making. However, failing to monitor and analyze variances can undermine the effectiveness of flexible budgeting, as organizations may miss opportunities for improvement or fail to address performance gaps.

Solution: Organizations should establish a systematic process for monitoring and analyzing variances. This involves regularly comparing actual results with the flexible budget and conducting detailed variance analysis to understand the reasons behind the discrepancies. By implementing a robust variance analysis process, organizations can identify trends, patterns, and potential areas for improvement, enabling proactive decision, making and performance enhancement.

Pitfall 4: Rigidity in Budget Adjustments

While flexible budgeting allows for adjustments based on changing activity levels, organizations may fall into the trap of rigidity, either by making insufficient adjustments or by overreacting to short, term fluctuations.

Solution: Organizations should strike a balance between making necessary adjustments and maintaining stability. This requires regularly reviewing and updating the flexible budget based on the changing business environment and activity levels. Implementing a continuous monitoring and adjustment process enables organizations to respond effectively to long, term trends while avoiding knee, jerk reactions to short, term fluctuations.

Pitfall 5: Lack of Training and Skill Development

Flexible budgeting requires financial acumen and analytical skills to effectively implement and interpret the results. However, organizations may face challenges if their employees lack the necessary training and skill development in flexible budgeting techniques and variance analysis.

Solution: Organizations should invest in training and skill development programs to equip employees with the necessary knowledge and expertise in flexible budgeting. This can include training on budgeting techniques, variance analysis, data interpretation, and financial acumen. By enhancing the capabilities of employees, organizations can ensure effective implementation of flexible budgeting and empower employees to make informed decisions based on the results.

Chapter Six

Flexible Budgets in Different Industries

Embracing Flexibility: The Application of Flexible Budgets in Different Industries

Flexible budgeting is a versatile financial management approach that can be adapted to various industries and sectors. The ability to adjust budgeted amounts based on changing activity levels makes flexible budgets an invaluable tool for organizations across different domains. Below we will explore the application of flexible budgets in different industries, highlighting their benefits and relevance in achieving financial objectives.

Manufacturing Industry:

In the manufacturing industry, where production volumes and costs can fluctuate significantly, flexible budgets play a crucial role in financial planning and control. Flexible budgets allow manufacturers to adjust their budgeted amounts based on changes in production levels, material costs, or labor expenses. This flexibility enables accurate performance evaluation, effective cost control, and efficient resource allocation. Manufacturers can analyze variances between actual results and the flexible budget to identify areas for improvement, streamline operations, and optimize production costs.

Retail Industry:

The retail industry is characterized by changing consumer behavior, seasonal demand, and market trends. Flexible budgets enable retailers to adapt to these fluctuations and optimize their financial performance. Retailers can adjust their budgeted amounts based on changes in sales volumes, pricing strategies, or promotional activities. This flexibility allows for accurate revenue assessment, effective cost management, and informed decision, making. By analyzing variances between actual results and the flexible budget, retailers can identify the drivers of performance, evaluate the success of marketing initiatives, and make data, driven decisions to enhance profitability.

Hospitality Industry:

In the hospitality industry, where demand can vary significantly based on seasons, events, or economic conditions, flexible budgets provide a valuable framework for financial planning and evaluation. Hospitality businesses, such as hotels or restaurants, can adjust their budgeted amounts based on changes in occupancy rates, average daily rates, or food and beverage costs. This adaptability enables accurate revenue forecasting, effective cost control, and improved profitability. By monitoring and analyzing variances between actual results and the flexible budget, hospitality businesses can identify opportunities to optimize revenue streams, manage costs, and enhance guest experiences.

Healthcare Industry:

Flexible budgets are particularly relevant in the healthcare industry, where patient volumes, medical expenses, and reimbursement rates can vary significantly. Healthcare providers can adjust their budgeted amounts based on changes in patient admissions, treatment costs, or regulatory requirements. This flexibility allows for accurate financial planning, effective resource allocation, and improved financial performance. By analyzing variances between actual results and the flexible budget, healthcare organizations can identify areas for cost savings, assess the impact of reimbursement changes, and make informed decisions to optimize patient care and financial outcomes.

Service Industry:

The service industry, encompassing sectors such as consulting, professional services, or technology, also benefits from the application of flexible budgets. Service, based organizations can adjust their budgeted amounts based on changes in project scope, client contracts, or resource utilization. This flexibility enables accurate revenue forecasting, effective cost management, and improved profitability. By monitoring variances between actual results and the flexible budget, service organizations can assess project profitability, allocate resources efficiently, and make data, driven decisions to enhance client satisfaction and financial performance.

Nonprofit Sector:

Flexible budgets are equally applicable in the nonprofit sector, where organizations aim to fulfill their mission within limited resources. Nonprofit organizations can adjust their budgeted amounts based on changes in funding sources, program requirements, or donor contributions. This adaptability allows for effective financial planning, transparent resource allocation, and improved sustainability. By analyzing variances between actual results and the flexible budget, nonprofits can evaluate the effectiveness of their programs, optimize fund allocation, and ensure compliance with funding restrictions.

Manufacturing Industry

Unleashing Potential: Flexible Budgeting in the Manufacturing Industry

The manufacturing industry is a dynamic sector characterized by ever, changing production volumes, fluctuating costs, and evolving market demands. In this fast, paced environment, effective financial management is crucial for success. Flexible budgeting emerges as a valuable tool for manufacturers to navigate these challenges, allowing them to adapt their budgeted amounts to the changing dynamics of the industry. Below we will explore the application of flexible budgeting in the manufacturing industry, highlighting its benefits and relevance in achieving financial objectives.

The Significance of Flexible Budgeting in the Manufacturing Industry:

Adapting to Fluctuating Production Volumes:

Manufacturers often face fluctuating production volumes due to changing market demands, seasonal variations, or economic factors. Fixed budgets, based on static assumptions, may become irrelevant in such circumstances. However, flexible budgeting allows manufacturers to adjust their budgeted amounts based on the actual level of production. This flexibility ensures that financial planning remains aligned with the changing production volumes, enabling accurate cost projections and revenue forecasts.

Effective Performance Evaluation:

Flexible budgeting plays a critical role in performance evaluation for manufacturers. By comparing actual results with the budgeted amounts adjusted for the actual production volumes, manufacturers can accurately assess their performance. Variances between actual results and the flexible budget provide insights into the effectiveness of production processes, cost control measures, and revenue generation strategies. This evaluation helps manufacturers identify areas for improvement, optimize resource allocation, and enhance operational efficiency.

Efficient Cost Control:

Cost control is a fundamental aspect of financial management in the manufacturing industry. Flexible budgeting allows manufacturers to monitor and control costs effectively. By comparing actual expenses with the budgeted amounts adjusted for the actual production volumes, manufacturers can identify cost, saving opportunities, pinpoint areas of cost overruns, and implement corrective actions. This proactive cost control approach ensures that expenses are aligned with production levels and helps manufacturers achieve greater profitability.

Optimized Resource Allocation:

Resource allocation is a critical decision for manufacturers, as they strive to utilize their resources efficiently. Flexible budgeting enables manufacturers to allocate resources effectively based on the actual production volumes. By adjusting the budgeted amounts to match the production levels, manufacturers can make informed decisions about labor deployment, raw material procurement, and equipment utilization. This optimization of resources leads to improved productivity, reduced waste, and enhanced operational performance.

Improved Cash Flow Management:

Cash flow management is vital for manufacturers to ensure smooth operations and meet financial obligations. Flexible budgeting aids in cash flow management by aligning budgeted amounts with the actual production volumes. This alignment enables manufacturers to project cash inflows and outflows accurately, facilitating proactive cash flow planning and minimizing cash flow constraints. Manufacturers can identify potential cash flow gaps, implement measures to bridge them, and ensure the availability of adequate working capital.

Support for Decision, Making:

Manufacturers frequently encounter complex decisions related to capacity expansion, product diversification, or investment in new technology. Flexible budgeting provides valuable insights for decision, making in such scenarios. By analyzing the variances between actual results and the flexible budget, manufacturers can evaluate the financial impact of different options and assess the feasibility of proposed initiatives. This analysis enables manufacturers to make data, driven decisions, allocate resources effectively, and seize opportunities for growth and innovation.

Enhanced Inventory Management:

Inventory management is a critical aspect of financial management in the manufacturing industry. By aligning the budgeted amounts with the actual production volumes, flexible budgeting helps manufacturers optimize their inventory levels. Manufacturers can accurately assess the inventory carrying costs, identify slow, moving or excess inventory, and adjust production and procurement plans accordingly. This improved inventory management ensures efficient working capital utilization and minimizes the risk of inventory obsolescence.

Service Industry

Adapting to Excellence: Flexible Budgeting in the Service Industry

The service industry encompasses a wide range of sectors, including consulting, professional services, technology, and hospitality. It is characterized by its intangible nature, a focus on client satisfaction, and the utilization of human capital. In this dynamic and competitive landscape, effective financial management is essential for success. Flexible budgeting emerges as a valuable tool for service, based organizations, enabling them to adapt their budgeted amounts to the changing dynamics of the industry. Below we will explore the application of flexible budgeting in the service industry, highlighting its benefits and relevance in achieving financial objectives.

The Role of Flexible Budgeting in the Service Industry:

Aligning Revenue Forecasting:

Flexible budgeting allows service, based organizations to align their revenue forecasts with the changing dynamics of the industry. By adjusting the budgeted amounts based on factors such as client contracts, project scope, or resource utilization, organizations can accurately project their revenue streams. This adaptability ensures that financial planning remains relevant and enables organizations to make informed decisions regarding resource allocation, investment priorities, and client acquisition strategies.

Resource Optimization:

Effective resource allocation is critical in the service industry, where human capital plays a central role. Flexible budgeting enables organizations to optimize their resource allocation by adjusting the budgeted amounts to match the demand for services. This adaptability ensures that the right resources are allocated to projects or client engagements, enhancing productivity, client satisfaction, and overall profitability. By aligning resource allocation with the actual level of demand, organizations can maximize their revenue generation potential.

Managing Variable Costs:

Variable costs are prevalent in the service industry, as they are directly linked to the volume of services provided. Flexible budgeting allows organizations to manage variable costs effectively by adjusting the budgeted amounts to match the level of service activity. This adaptability enables accurate cost projections, better cost control, and improved profitability.

By monitoring and analyzing variances between actual results and the flexible budget, organizations can identify areas for cost savings, streamline operations, and enhance overall efficiency.

Enhancing Project Profitability:

In the service industry, profitability is closely tied to the success of individual projects or client engagements. Flexible budgeting facilitates accurate project profitability assessment by aligning the budgeted amounts with the specific requirements of each project. By monitoring and analyzing variances between actual results and the flexible budget, organizations can evaluate the financial performance of each project, identify areas for improvement, and make informed decisions to enhance profitability. This analysis allows organizations to optimize pricing strategies, manage project costs, and ensure that resources are utilized efficiently.

Effective Cash Flow Management:

Cash flow management is crucial for service, based organizations to maintain their operations and meet financial obligations. Flexible budgeting aids in cash flow management by aligning budgeted amounts with the actual level of service activity. This alignment enables organizations to project cash inflows and outflows accurately, facilitating proactive cash flow planning and minimizing cash flow constraints. By analyzing variances between actual results and the flexible budget, organizations can identify potential cash flow gaps, implement measures to bridge them, and ensure the availability of adequate working capital.

Strategic Decision, Making:

Flexible budgeting supports strategic decision, making by providing timely and accurate financial information. Performance evaluation based on flexible budgets helps organizations identify trends, patterns, and potential opportunities. By aligning financial results with strategic objectives, organizations can make informed decisions regarding investment priorities, growth strategies, and service portfolio expansion. The insights gained from performance evaluation contribute to the formulation of effective strategies that drive profitability and support long, term success.

Retail Industry

Thriving in Change: Flexible Budgeting in the Retail Industry

The retail industry is a dynamic and competitive sector, constantly influenced by changing consumer behavior, market trends, and economic conditions. In this fast, paced environment, effective financial management is essential for success. Flexible budgeting emerges as a valuable tool for retailers, enabling them to adapt their budgeted amounts to the ever, changing dynamics of the industry. Below we will explore the application of flexible budgeting in the retail industry, highlighting its benefits and relevance in achieving financial objectives.

The Role of Flexible Budgeting in the Retail Industry:

Aligning Revenue Projections:

Flexible budgeting allows retailers to align their revenue projections with the dynamic nature of the industry. By adjusting the budgeted amounts based on factors such as sales volumes, pricing strategies, or promotional activities, retailers can accurately forecast their revenue streams. This adaptability ensures that financial planning remains relevant and enables retailers to make informed decisions regarding inventory management, marketing investments, and overall business strategies.

Effective Cost Management:

Cost management is critical for retailers to maintain profitability and sustain business growth. Flexible budgeting enables retailers to manage costs effectively by adjusting the budgeted amounts to match the level of sales activity. This adaptability ensures that cost projections are aligned with the revenue potential, allowing retailers to optimize their cost structure, reduce inefficiencies, and enhance profitability. By monitoring and analyzing variances between actual results and the flexible budget, retailers can identify areas for cost savings, streamline operations, and improve overall cost control.

Inventory Optimization:

Inventory management is a key aspect of financial management in the retail industry. Flexible budgeting supports retailers in optimizing their inventory levels by adjusting the budgeted amounts to match the expected sales volumes. This adaptability allows retailers to project accurate inventory carrying costs, identify slow, moving or excess inventory, and adjust procurement plans accordingly. Effective inventory optimization ensures efficient working capital utilization, minimizes the risk of inventory obsolescence, and improves overall cash flow management.

Enhancing Pricing Strategies:

Flexible budgeting enables retailers to evaluate and refine their pricing strategies accurately. By monitoring variances between actual results and the flexible budget, retailers can assess the effectiveness of their pricing initiatives and make data, driven decisions to optimize pricing. This analysis helps retailers identify the impact of pricing changes on profitability, evaluate competitive dynamics, and adjust pricing strategies accordingly. By aligning pricing decisions with financial outcomes, retailers can strike a balance between maximizing revenue and maintaining customer satisfaction.

Promotional Campaign Evaluation:

Promotional campaigns play a significant role in the retail industry, aiming to drive sales and attract customers. Flexible budgeting facilitates the evaluation of promotional campaigns by adjusting the budgeted amounts to reflect the expected impact on sales. By analyzing variances between actual results and the flexible budget, retailers can assess the effectiveness of promotional activities, evaluate return on investment (ROI), and make informed decisions about future promotional initiatives. This analysis allows retailers to allocate resources effectively and focus on activities that deliver the most significant financial impact.

Facilitating Decision, Making:

Flexible budgeting supports strategic decision, making in the retail industry. By providing timely and accurate financial information, performance evaluation based on flexible budgets helps retailers identify trends, patterns, and potential opportunities. This information facilitates data, driven decision, making regarding store expansion, product assortment, supplier negotiations, and investment priorities. The insights gained from performance evaluation contribute to the formulation of effective strategies that align with market dynamics and customer preferences.

Adapting to Consumer Behavior:

Consumer behavior is constantly evolving, influenced by factors such as economic conditions, technological advancements, and social trends. Flexible budgeting allows retailers to adapt to these changes by adjusting the budgeted amounts to reflect shifting consumer preferences and demands. This adaptability ensures that financial planning remains aligned with the market dynamics, enabling retailers to capitalize on emerging opportunities,

Chapter Seven

Case Studies: Flexible Budgeting in Practice

Unveiling Success Stories: Case Studies of Flexible Budgeting in Practice

Flexible budgeting is a powerful financial management approach that allows organizations to adapt their budgeted amounts to changing circumstances. While the theoretical benefits of flexible budgeting are well, established, examining real, world case studies can provide practical insights into its application and effectiveness. Below we will explore case studies of organizations that have successfully implemented flexible budgeting, highlighting their experiences, outcomes, and the lessons we can learn from their journey.

Case Study 1: Company X , Manufacturing Industry

Company X is a manufacturing company that produces consumer electronics. To navigate the dynamic market conditions and fluctuating production volumes, the company implemented flexible budgeting. By adjusting the budgeted amounts based on the actual production levels, Company X achieved several benefits. First, accurate performance evaluation became possible, as the flexible budget aligned with the achieved activity levels. This allowed the company to identify areas of efficiency, make informed decisions, and take corrective actions. Second, the ability to analyze variances between actual results and the flexible budget helped Company X identify cost, saving opportunities and optimize resource allocation.

As a result, the company improved its cost control, reduced waste, and increased profitability. The successful implementation of flexible budgeting empowered Company X to thrive in a competitive manufacturing industry.

Case Study 2: Company Y , Service Industry

Company Y is a consulting firm that provides management advisory services. In a highly competitive and client, driven service industry, Company Y recognized the importance of aligning financial planning with the actual demand for services. By adopting flexible budgeting, the company adjusted its budgeted amounts based on project scope, client contracts, and resource utilization. This approach enabled Company Y to optimize resource allocation, enhance project profitability, and improve cash flow management. The ability to monitor variances between actual results and the flexible budget allowed the company to identify areas for improvement, refine pricing strategies, and make informed decisions about future projects. The successful implementation of flexible budgeting contributed to Company Y's growth, client satisfaction, and financial success.

Case Study 3: Company Z , Retail Industry

Company Z is a retail chain operating in the fashion industry. The company faced challenges related to fluctuating sales volumes, seasonal variations, and evolving consumer preferences. To address these challenges, Company Z implemented flexible budgeting. By adjusting the budgeted amounts based on sales volumes, pricing strategies, and promotional activities, the company gained several advantages. First, it achieved accurate revenue forecasting, allowing for effective inventory management and resource allocation. Second, the ability to analyze variances between actual results and the flexible budget enabled Company Z to evaluate the impact of pricing and promotional initiatives, optimize pricing strategies, and enhance profitability. The successful implementation of flexible budgeting empowered Company Z to adapt to changing market conditions, drive sales growth, and stay competitive in the retail industry.

Lessons Learned:

From these case studies, several key lessons can be derived:

Alignment with Actual Activity Levels: The success of flexible budgeting lies in aligning the budgeted amounts with the actual activity levels achieved. This ensures accurate performance evaluation, facilitates effective cost control, and optimizes resource allocation.

Variances as Insights: Analyzing variances between actual results and the flexible budget provides valuable insights for decision, making. It helps identify areas for improvement, cost, saving opportunities, and growth potential.

Continuous Monitoring and Adaptation: Flexible budgeting is an ongoing process that requires continuous monitoring and adaptation. Regularly reviewing and adjusting the budgeted amounts based on changing circumstances ensures its effectiveness and relevance.

Small Business Scenario

Thriving against the Odds: A Small Business Scenario and the Power of Flexible Budgeting

Small businesses face unique challenges in today's competitive market. Limited resources, fluctuating customer demand, and operational uncertainties often test their resilience. In this scenario, effective financial management becomes crucial for survival and growth. Flexible budgeting emerges as a powerful tool that small businesses can leverage to navigate these challenges. Below we will explore a small business scenario and illustrate how flexible budgeting can play a vital role in its success.

The Small Business Scenario:

Imagine a small bakery named Sweet Delights. It is a family, owned business specializing in artisanal cakes, pastries, and desserts. Sweet Delights has been operating for two years and has established a loyal customer base. However, it faces several financial challenges typical of small businesses, such as limited working capital, fluctuating sales volumes, and uncertain costs.

Application of Flexible Budgeting:

Sweet Delights decides to implement flexible budgeting to address these challenges and improve its financial performance. Here's how flexible budgeting proves beneficial in various aspects of the business:

Accurate Revenue Forecasting:

Flexible budgeting allows Sweet Delights to align its revenue projections with the actual sales volumes. By adjusting the budgeted amounts based on seasonal variations, market trends, and customer preferences, the bakery can accurately forecast its revenue streams. This adaptability enables Sweet Delights to make informed decisions about pricing strategies, product offerings, and marketing initiatives, ensuring optimal revenue generation.

Effective Cost Management:

Cost management is crucial for small businesses, where efficient resource allocation and cost control are essential for profitability. Flexible budgeting empowers Sweet Delights to manage its costs effectively. By adjusting the budgeted amounts based on actual sales volumes and cost drivers, the bakery can accurately project its expenses. Monitoring and analyzing variances between actual results and the flexible budget enable Sweet Delights to identify cost, saving opportunities, streamline operations, and optimize its cost structure, enhancing overall profitability.

Cash Flow Optimization:

Cash flow management is a significant concern for small businesses, as they often face irregular income and expenses. Flexible budgeting assists Sweet Delights in optimizing its cash flow. By aligning the budgeted amounts with the actual sales volumes and payment cycles, the bakery can project its cash inflows and outflows accurately. This adaptability helps Sweet Delights anticipate potential cash flow gaps, plan for working capital needs, and make informed decisions to ensure a healthy cash position.

Inventory Control:

Inventory management is critical for businesses like Sweet Delights, where the freshness and quality of products directly impact customer satisfaction. Flexible budgeting enables the bakery to optimize its inventory levels. By adjusting the budgeted amounts to match the expected sales volumes and inventory turnover rates, Sweet Delights can manage its inventory effectively. This adaptability helps the bakery minimize waste, reduce carrying costs, and ensure that the right products are available at the right time, improving customer service and financial performance.

Strategic Decision, Making:

Strategic decision, making is essential for the long, term success of small businesses. Flexible budgeting supports Sweet Delights in making strategic decisions by providing timely and accurate financial information. Performance evaluation based on flexible budgets helps the bakery identify trends, patterns, and potential opportunities. This information assists Sweet Delights in formulating effective strategies related to product expansion, target markets, marketing investments, and operational improvements.

Corporate Scenario

Unleashing Agility: Flexible Budgeting in a Corporate Scenario

In today's fast, paced and ever, changing corporate landscape, effective financial management is crucial for organizational success. Corporations face numerous challenges, such as market uncertainties, changing customer preferences, and volatile economic conditions. In this scenario, flexible budgeting emerges as a powerful tool that corporations can leverage to navigate these challenges. Below we will explore a corporate scenario and illustrate how flexible budgeting can play a vital role in its financial management.

The Corporate Scenario:

Imagine a multinational technology company named TechGenius. It operates in a highly competitive market, constantly striving to innovate and meet customer demands. TechGenius faces financial challenges inherent in large corporations, such as complex cost structures, dynamic revenue streams, and the need for effective resource allocation.

Application of Flexible Budgeting:

TechGenius recognizes the need for agility in its financial management and decides to implement flexible budgeting. Let's explore how flexible budgeting proves beneficial in various aspects of the corporate scenario:

Revenue Forecasting and Market Adaptation:

Flexible budgeting allows TechGenius to align its revenue projections with market dynamics. By adjusting the budgeted amounts based on changing customer preferences, market trends, and product lifecycles, the company can accurately forecast its revenue streams. This adaptability empowers TechGenius to make informed decisions about investment priorities, product development, and market expansion, ensuring sustained revenue growth.

Effective Cost Control and Resource Optimization:

Cost control is essential for large corporations, where complex cost structures can challenge profitability. Flexible budgeting enables TechGenius to manage its costs effectively. By adjusting the budgeted amounts based on actual performance, market conditions, and cost drivers, the company can accurately project its expenses. Monitoring and analyzing variances between actual results and the flexible budget enable TechGenius to identify cost, saving opportunities, streamline operations, and optimize resource allocation, enhancing overall profitability.

Capital Expenditure Planning:

Large corporations often face significant capital expenditure decisions, such as investments in research and development, infrastructure, or acquisitions. Flexible budgeting supports TechGenius in making informed capital expenditure decisions. By aligning the budgeted amounts with strategic objectives and market opportunities, the company can evaluate the financial impact of different investment options. This adaptability helps TechGenius allocate its capital effectively, minimize risk, and enhance return on investment.

Cash Flow Management and Working Capital Optimization:

Cash flow management is critical for corporations to ensure their financial stability and meet operational needs. Flexible budgeting assists TechGenius in optimizing its cash flow. By aligning the budgeted amounts with the actual revenue streams and payment cycles, the company can project its cash inflows and outflows accurately. This adaptability helps TechGenius anticipate potential cash flow gaps, plan for working capital needs, and make informed decisions to maintain a healthy cash position.

Performance Evaluation and Decision, Making:

Flexible budgeting provides TechGenius with a framework for performance evaluation and decision, making. By comparing actual results with the flexible budget, the company can identify areas of success, challenges, and potential opportunities. This analysis supports data, driven decision, making, as TechGenius can align financial outcomes with strategic objectives, evaluate the effectiveness of various initiatives, and adjust its course accordingly.

Risk Management:

Corporations operate in an environment characterized by inherent risks, including market volatility, technological disruptions, and regulatory changes. Flexible budgeting assists TechGenius in managing risks effectively. By adjusting the budgeted amounts based on risk assessment and market uncertainties, the company can build contingency plans and allocate resources strategically. This adaptability helps TechGenius mitigate potential risks, maintain financial stability, and seize opportunities amidst uncertainty.

Non

,

profit Organization Scenario

Embracing Flexibility: Flexible Budgeting in a Non, profit Organization Scenario

Non, profit organizations play a vital role in addressing social challenges, supporting communities, and driving positive change. However, these organizations face unique financial management challenges, including limited resources, donor expectations, and the need for transparent and accountable financial practices. In this scenario, flexible budgeting emerges as a powerful tool that non, profit organizations can leverage to navigate these challenges effectively. Below we will explore a non, profit organization scenario and illustrate how flexible budgeting can play a vital role in its financial management.

The Non, profit Organization Scenario:

Imagine a non, profit organization named CareWorks, dedicated to providing educational support and healthcare services to underprivileged communities. CareWorks operates with limited funds and relies heavily on donor contributions and grants to support its programs. The organization faces financial challenges inherent in the non, profit sector, such as donor fluctuations, grant restrictions, and the need for efficient resource allocation.

Application of Flexible Budgeting:

CareWorks recognizes the importance of flexibility in its financial management and decides to implement flexible budgeting. Let's explore how flexible budgeting proves beneficial in various aspects of the non, profit organization scenario:

Donor Contribution and Grant Management:

Flexible budgeting allows CareWorks to align its budgeted amounts with donor contributions and grant restrictions. By adjusting the budgeted amounts based on the actual funding received and specific program requirements, the organization can effectively manage its resources. This adaptability ensures that financial planning remains aligned with available funds, enabling CareWorks to meet its program objectives and maintain donor trust.

Program Evaluation and Impact Assessment:

Non, profit organizations must demonstrate the impact of their programs to stakeholders and donors. Flexible budgeting supports CareWorks in evaluating program effectiveness and assessing its impact. By analyzing variances between actual results and the flexible budget, the organization can identify program successes, challenges, and areas for improvement. This analysis helps CareWorks refine its programs, allocate resources effectively, and ensure that donor funds are utilized in a transparent and accountable manner.

Cost Control and Resource Allocation:

Non, profit organizations strive to maximize their impact while operating within limited resources. Flexible budgeting enables CareWorks to control costs effectively and optimize resource allocation. By adjusting the budgeted amounts based on program needs, operational costs, and fundraising activities, the organization can ensure efficient resource utilization. Monitoring and analyzing variances between actual results and the flexible budget empower CareWorks to identify cost, saving opportunities, streamline operations, and allocate resources strategically to enhance its programs' reach and effectiveness.

Cash Flow Management and Sustainability:

Cash flow management is crucial for non, profit organizations to maintain their operations and sustain their impact. Flexible budgeting assists Care-

Works in optimizing its cash flow. By aligning the budgeted amounts with the actual cash inflows and outflows, the organization can project its cash flow needs accurately. This adaptability helps CareWorks anticipate potential cash flow gaps, plan for fundraising activities, and make informed decisions to ensure its long, term sustainability and program continuity.

Grant Proposal and Fundraising Strategies:

Non, profit organizations heavily rely on grants and fundraising efforts to support their programs. Flexible budgeting supports CareWorks in developing grant proposals and fundraising strategies. By aligning the budgeted amounts with specific grant requirements and fundraising targets, the organization can accurately project its financial needs. This adaptability helps CareWorks present a compelling case to potential funders, demonstrate its financial viability, and enhance its chances of securing grants and attracting donors.

Chapter Eight

Advanced Topics in Flexible Budgeting

Exploring New Horizons: Advanced Topics in Flexible Budgeting

Flexible budgeting has proven to be a valuable tool for organizations across various sectors, enabling them to adapt their budgeted amounts to changing circumstances. As organizations strive for continuous improvement in financial management, advanced topics in flexible budgeting offer new insights and approaches. Below we will delve into advanced topics in flexible budgeting, exploring concepts and techniques that enhance its effectiveness and provide organizations with a competitive edge.

Rolling Budgets:

Traditional budgeting often involves preparing annual budgets, which may become obsolete as the year progresses. Rolling budgets address this limitation by continuously updating the budget for future periods. This approach allows organizations to incorporate new information, adjust forecasts, and align financial planning with changing circumstances. Rolling budgets provide greater flexibility and enable organizations to make timely decisions based on up, to, date financial projections.

Beyond Financial Metrics:

While financial metrics are essential in budgeting, advanced flexible budgeting techniques consider non, financial metrics as well. Organizations can incorporate key performance indicators (KPIs) related to customer satisfaction, employee productivity, sustainability, and innovation. By including non, financial metrics, organizations gain a holistic view of performance, enabling them to make informed decisions that align with their broader goals and values.

Scenario Planning:

Scenario planning involves developing multiple scenarios based on different assumptions and events that may impact an organization's performance. Advanced flexible budgeting incorporates scenario planning to assess the financial implications of various future scenarios. By analyzing different scenarios, organizations can evaluate potential risks, identify opportunities, and develop contingency plans. Scenario planning enhances decision, making by providing insights into potential outcomes and enabling organizations to proactively respond to changing circumstances.

Sensitivity Analysis:

Sensitivity analysis helps organizations understand the impact of changes in key variables on their financial performance. Advanced flexible budgeting includes sensitivity analysis to assess the sensitivity of budgeted amounts to changes in factors such as sales volumes, pricing, costs, or market conditions. By quantifying the potential impact of these variables, organizations can evaluate their risk exposure and develop strategies to mitigate uncertainties. Sensitivity analysis enhances financial planning by providing a more comprehensive understanding of the organization's vulnerabilities and opportunities.

Activity, Based Budgeting:

Activity, based budgeting (ABB) focuses on understanding the cost drivers and resource requirements for various activities within an organization. This approach allows organizations to allocate resources based on the activities that contribute the most value. Advanced flexible budgeting incorporates ABB to align budgeted amounts with the specific activities and projects that drive organizational success. By prioritizing resources according to activity, based insights, organizations can optimize their resource allocation, enhance efficiency, and maximize their return on investment.

Zero, Based Budgeting:

Zero, based budgeting (ZBB) challenges the traditional approach of incremental budgeting by requiring organizations to justify every expense from scratch, regardless of prior budget allocations. Advanced flexible budgeting embraces ZBB to encourage a thorough review of all expenses and align them with strategic priorities. By reevaluating each expense item, organizations can identify areas of inefficiency, eliminate wasteful spending, and allocate resources to high, value initiatives. ZBB promotes cost, consciousness and enhances resource optimization within organizations.

Integrated Financial Planning:

Advanced flexible budgeting emphasizes the integration of financial planning with other organizational processes, such as strategic planning and performance management. By aligning financial goals with strategic objectives, organizations can ensure that budgeted amounts support the realization of their long, term vision. Integrated financial planning fosters synergy across different functions and promotes a comprehensive view of organizational performance. It facilitates effective decision, making, encourages collaboration, and enhances organizational agility.

Integrating Flexible Budgeting with Standard Costing

Synergy Unleashed: Integrating Flexible Budgeting with Standard Costing

Financial management requires organizations to employ various tools and techniques to effectively plan, control, and evaluate their operations. Two commonly used approaches in this realm are flexible budgeting and standard costing. While both methods have their merits, integrating them can lead to powerful synergies. Below we will explore the integration of flexible budgeting with standard costing, highlighting its benefits, applications, and implications for organizational financial management.

Understanding Flexible Budgeting:

Flexible budgeting is a dynamic approach that allows organizations to adjust budgeted amounts based on changes in activity levels or volume. It provides a more accurate reflection of expected costs and revenues by considering the actual level of production or activity. Flexible budgeting is particularly useful in industries with variable costs, where it enables organizations to respond effectively to changing market conditions and operational requirements.

Understanding Standard Costing:

Standard costing is a method that establishes predetermined costs for various inputs, such as materials, labor, and overheads, based on historical data and industry benchmarks. It serves as a benchmark against which actual costs are compared, allowing organizations to evaluate variances and identify areas of inefficiency or cost overruns. Standard costing provides a basis for cost control, performance evaluation, and decision, making within organizations.

Integration of Flexible Budgeting and Standard Costing:

When flexible budgeting and standard costing are integrated, organizations can benefit from a comprehensive financial management system that combines the advantages of both approaches. Let's explore the key aspects of this integration:

Accurate Costing:

Standard costing provides predetermined costs for inputs based on historical data, while flexible budgeting adjusts budgeted amounts based on the actual level of activity. By integrating these approaches, organizations can achieve more accurate costing. The predetermined costs of standard costing provide a benchmark for comparison with actual costs, enabling organizations to identify cost variances and take appropriate corrective actions. The adjustment of budgeted amounts in flexible budgeting ensures that costs are aligned with the actual level of activity, providing a more accurate reflection of the cost structure.

Variances Analysis:

Integrating flexible budgeting with standard costing enhances variances analysis. Standard costing provides the expected cost benchmarks, and flexible budgeting adjusts those benchmarks based on the actual level of activity. By comparing actual costs with the adjusted benchmarks, organizations can analyze variances in a more meaningful way. This analysis helps identify the causes of cost variances and supports decision, making regarding cost control, process improvement, and resource allocation.

Performance Evaluation:

The integration of flexible budgeting with standard costing strengthens performance evaluation. Standard costing establishes performance benchmarks, and flexible budgeting adjusts those benchmarks based on the actual level of activity. By comparing actual performance with the adjusted benchmarks, organizations can assess their operational efficiency and effectiveness. This evaluation enables organizations to identify areas of improvement, set realistic performance targets, and align their efforts with strategic goals.

Cost Control and Continuous Improvement:

Integrating flexible budgeting with standard costing enhances cost control and supports continuous improvement efforts. Standard costing provides a basis for cost planning, and flexible budgeting adjusts the budgeted amounts to reflect the actual level of activity. By monitoring cost variances and analyzing their causes, organizations can identify areas of inefficiency, implement cost, saving measures, and drive continuous improvement initiatives. This integration promotes a culture of cost consciousness and supports the pursuit of operational excellence.

Decision, Making:

The integration of flexible budgeting with standard costing enhances decision, making within organizations. The combination of historical cost benchmarks from standard costing and adjusted budgeted amounts from flexible budgeting provides a comprehensive view of the financial implications of different decisions. This integrated approach enables organizations to make informed decisions regarding pricing strategies, resource allocation, product mix, and investment priorities.

Flexible Budgeting for Capital Expenditures

Embracing Flexibility: Flexible Budgeting for Capital Expenditures

Capital expenditures play a crucial role in the growth and development of organizations. Whether it's investing in new technology, expanding facilities, or acquiring assets, effective financial management is essential to ensure the success of capital projects. Flexible budgeting offers a valuable approach to navigate the uncertainties and complexities associated with capital expenditures. Below we will explore the application of flexible budgeting for capital expenditures, highlighting its benefits and significance in financial decision, making.

Understanding Capital Expenditures:

Capital expenditures, also known as CapEx, refer to investments made by organizations to acquire, improve, or maintain long, term assets. These expenditures involve substantial financial commitments and have a significant impact on an organization's financial health and future prospects. Proper evaluation and management of capital expenditures are crucial to ensure optimal resource allocation and maximize return on investment.

The Role of Flexible Budgeting in Capital Expenditures:

Flexible budgeting plays a vital role in capital expenditure management, providing organizations with the ability to adjust budgeted amounts based on changing circumstances and actual performance. Here's how flexible budgeting enhances the decision, making process for capital expenditures:

Accurate Cost Estimation:

Flexible budgeting allows organizations to accurately estimate the costs associated with capital expenditures. By considering factors such as inflation, market conditions, and project, specific requirements, organizations can adjust the budgeted amounts to reflect the actual costs involved. This adaptability ensures that cost estimates are realistic and aligned with the prevailing economic conditions, reducing the risk of cost overruns and facilitating better financial planning.

Risk Assessment and Contingency Planning:

Capital projects often involve inherent risks, such as unexpected delays, cost escalations, or regulatory changes. Flexible budgeting enables organizations to incorporate risk assessment and contingency planning into their capital expenditure budgets. By adjusting the budgeted amounts to account for potential risks and uncertainties, organizations can allocate resources for contingency measures and minimize the adverse impact of unforeseen events. This proactive approach to risk management enhances financial resilience and mitigates potential disruptions in capital projects.

Adjusting Investment Criteria:

Flexible budgeting allows organizations to adjust their investment criteria based on changing market conditions and strategic objectives. By adjusting the budgeted amounts to reflect revised assumptions, growth projections, or market dynamics, organizations can align their investment decisions with their evolving priorities. This adaptability enables organizations to seize new opportunities, respond to competitive pressures, and allocate resources to projects with the highest potential for value creation.

Performance Evaluation:

Flexible budgeting provides a framework for performance evaluation in capital expenditure projects. By comparing actual results with the adjusted budgeted amounts, organizations can analyze variances, assess project performance, and identify areas for improvement. This evaluation facilitates informed decision, making, as organizations can make adjustments, reallocate resources, or take corrective actions based on actual performance data. By monitoring project progress against the flexible budget, organizations can ensure that capital expenditure projects remain on track and deliver the expected financial outcomes.

Resource Optimization:

Flexible budgeting enables organizations to optimize resource allocation in capital expenditure projects. By adjusting the budgeted amounts based on project, specific requirements, resource availability, and strategic priorities, organizations can allocate resources more efficiently. This adaptability ensures that resources are directed towards critical project components, reducing waste, and enhancing overall cost, effectiveness. Resource optimization contributes to improved project outcomes and enhances financial performance.

Cash Flow Management:

Capital expenditure projects often involve significant cash outflows over an extended period. Flexible budgeting helps organizations manage their cash flow effectively by adjusting the budgeted amounts to reflect the timing and magnitude of cash flows associated with capital projects. This adaptability enables organizations to plan their cash flow requirements, anticipate funding needs, and explore financing options to ensure uninterrupted project progress.

Zero

,

Based Budgeting vs. Flexible Budgeting

Exploring Financial Management Strategies: Zero, Based Budgeting vs. Flexible Budgeting

Financial management strategies play a crucial role in guiding organizations towards financial stability, efficiency, and growth. Among the various approaches available, zero, based budgeting (ZBB) and flexible budgeting are two prominent methods that organizations can employ. While both strategies aim to optimize resource allocation and enhance financial performance, they differ in their approach and application. Below we will compare and contrast zero, based budgeting and flexible budgeting, highlighting their key features, benefits, and implications for financial decision, making.

Understanding Zero, Based Budgeting:

Zero, based budgeting is an approach that requires organizations to justify and allocate resources from scratch, regardless of prior budget allocations. Under this method, every expense item must be evaluated and justified based on its necessity and alignment with strategic objectives. Zero, based budgeting breaks away from the incremental budgeting approach, which assumes that the previous year's budget is a reasonable starting point for the current year.

Understanding Flexible Budgeting:

Flexible budgeting is a dynamic approach that adjusts budgeted amounts based on changes in activity levels or volume. It provides organizations with the flexibility to adapt their budgeted amounts to actual performance levels or changes in market conditions. Flexible budgeting allows for more accurate financial planning and performance evaluation by aligning budgeted amounts with the achieved activity levels or changes in business operations.

Comparison of Zero, Based Budgeting and Flexible Budgeting:

Approach:

Zero, Based Budgeting: ZBB requires organizations to justify all expenses from scratch, starting each budgeting cycle with a clean slate. It focuses on the need for each expense and evaluates its contribution to organizational objectives. ZBB encourages a thorough review of expenses, aiming to eliminate inefficiencies and optimize resource allocation.

Flexible Budgeting: Flexible budgeting adjusts budgeted amounts based on changes in activity levels or volume. It allows organizations to adapt their budgeted amounts to actual performance levels, taking into account changes in business operations or market conditions. Flexible budgeting promotes accuracy and relevance in financial planning and performance evaluation.

Resource Allocation:

Zero, Based Budgeting: ZBB emphasizes optimizing resource allocation by evaluating the necessity and impact of each expense. It encourages organizations to allocate resources based on value creation and strategic priorities. ZBB challenges the status quo and ensures that resources are allocated efficiently and effectively.

Flexible Budgeting: Flexible budgeting enables organizations to allocate resources based on actual performance levels or changes in business operations. It ensures that resources are aligned with achieved activity levels and allows for adjustments in resource allocation as per changing circumstances.

Cost Control:

Zero, Based Budgeting: ZBB promotes cost control by requiring organizations to justify every expense. It encourages a critical evaluation of costs and drives cost reduction efforts. ZBB aims to eliminate unnecessary expenses and identifies opportunities for cost, saving measures.

Flexible Budgeting: Flexible budgeting supports cost control by adjusting budgeted amounts to reflect the achieved activity levels. It enables organizations to monitor variances between actual results and the flexible budget, identifying areas of cost overruns or cost savings opportunities.

Flexible budgeting facilitates effective cost management and optimization of resource allocation.

Performance Evaluation:

Zero, Based Budgeting: ZBB provides a comprehensive framework for performance evaluation. By evaluating expenses based on their alignment with strategic objectives, ZBB helps organizations assess the efficiency and effectiveness of resource utilization. It facilitates performance, based decision, making and fosters accountability.

Flexible Budgeting: Flexible budgeting enhances performance evaluation by aligning budgeted amounts with the achieved activity levels. Organizations can compare actual results with the flexible budget, analyze variances, and identify areas of improvement or efficiency. Flexible budgeting enables organizations to evaluate their performance accurately and make informed decisions based on actual performance data.

Chapter Nine

The Role of Technology in Flexible Budgeting

Empowering Financial Agility: The Role of Technology in Flexible Budgeting

In today's digital age, technology has become an integral part of organizational operations across various industries. The realm of financial management is no exception. Technology has revolutionized the way organizations approach financial planning, budgeting, and decision, making. In the context of flexible budgeting, technology plays a crucial role in enhancing its effectiveness and efficiency. Below we will explore the role of technology in flexible budgeting, highlighting its benefits, applications, and implications for financial management.

Automated Data Collection and Integration:

Technology enables organizations to automate the collection and integration of financial data, a fundamental requirement for flexible budgeting. With the use of advanced accounting software and systems, organizations can streamline data gathering from various sources such as sales, expenses, and production. This automation eliminates manual data entry errors and ensures the accuracy and consistency of financial information. By integrating data seamlessly, organizations can develop more comprehensive and reliable flexible budgets.

Real, Time Data Analysis:

Technology provides organizations with the capability to analyze financial data in real, time, enhancing the timeliness and effectiveness of flexible budgeting. Through powerful data analytics tools and dashboards, organizations can monitor key financial metrics, track performance, and analyze variances between actual results and the flexible budget. Real, time data analysis enables organizations to make timely adjustments, identify emerging trends, and take proactive measures to address financial challenges or exploit opportunities.

Scenario Planning and Forecasting:

Technology facilitates advanced scenario planning and forecasting, enhancing the predictive capabilities of flexible budgeting. Through sophisticated modeling and simulation tools, organizations can develop multiple scenarios based on different assumptions and variables. These scenarios enable organizations to anticipate potential outcomes, assess the financial impact of different decisions, and evaluate risks and opportunities. Technology, enabled scenario planning enhances the accuracy and relevance of flexible budgeting, enabling organizations to make informed decisions based on future projections.

Collaborative Budgeting Processes:

Technology enables organizations to implement collaborative budgeting processes, promoting cross, functional collaboration and participation. Web, based budgeting software and cloud, based platforms allow stakeholders from different departments and locations to contribute to the budgeting process. Collaborative budgeting fosters transparency, communication, and engagement, ensuring that diverse perspectives are incorporated into the flexible budget. This inclusive approach improves the accuracy and acceptance of the budget, enhancing its effectiveness in financial management.

Resource Allocation and Optimization:

Technology empowers organizations to optimize resource allocation through advanced algorithms and optimization models. By leveraging artificial intelligence and machine learning techniques, organizations can identify optimal resource allocation strategies based on various constraints and objectives. This optimization process ensures that resources are allocated efficiently and effectively, maximizing their utilization and minimizing waste. Technology, driven resource allocation supports the effectiveness of flexible budgeting by aligning resources with the achieved activity levels and strategic priorities.

Integrated Financial Management Systems:

Technology facilitates the integration of financial management systems, enabling seamless coordination between budgeting, accounting, and performance management processes. Integrated systems ensure that financial information flows smoothly across different functions, eliminating data silos and enhancing the accuracy and reliability of financial reports. This integration enables organizations to have a holistic view of financial performance, ensuring that the flexible budget aligns with organizational objectives and financial realities.

Mobile Accessibility and Remote Collaboration:

Technology enables mobile accessibility and remote collaboration, allowing organizations to conduct flexible budgeting processes efficiently, even in distributed work environments. With the use of mobile applications and cloud, based platforms, stakeholders can access financial data, review budgets, and participate in discussions from anywhere at any time. Mobile accessibility and remote collaboration ensure the continuity and efficiency of the budgeting process, regardless of physical location or time constraints.

Using Spreadsheet Software for Flexible Budgeting

Unleashing the Power of Spreadsheets: Using Spreadsheet Software for Flexible Budgeting

In the realm of financial management, organizations rely on various tools and techniques to optimize their budgeting processes. One such tool that has become indispensable in modern financial operations is spreadsheet software. With its versatility and analytical capabilities, spreadsheet software has revolutionized the way organizations approach budgeting, including flexible budgeting. Below we will explore the benefits, applications, and implications of using spreadsheet software for flexible budgeting, highlighting its role in enhancing accuracy, efficiency, and decision, making.

Data Organization and Structure:

Spreadsheet software provides organizations with a structured framework for organizing financial data, making it an ideal platform for flexible budgeting. By using columns to represent different expense categories or revenue sources and rows to represent various periods or activity levels, organizations can create a structured and intuitive layout for their flexible budgets. This organization facilitates data entry, review, and analysis, ensuring that budgeted amounts are accurately allocated to the appropriate categories and periods.

Calculation and Formulas:

Spreadsheet software offers a wide range of mathematical and statistical functions that simplify calculations and automate data analysis. Organizations can use formulas to perform complex calculations, such as summing up expenses, calculating variances, or forecasting future values based on historical data. By leveraging the calculation capabilities of spreadsheet software, organizations can ensure accurate and consistent calculations within their flexible budgets. This automation saves time and reduces the risk of manual errors, enhancing the reliability of budgeted amounts.

Sensitivity Analysis and What, If Scenarios:

Flexible budgeting involves assessing the impact of changes in activity levels or other variables on financial outcomes. Spreadsheet software enables organizations to conduct sensitivity analysis and explore different what, if scenarios to evaluate the financial implications of various changes. By adjusting input values in the spreadsheet and observing the resulting changes in budgeted amounts, organizations can assess the sensitivity of their budgets and make informed decisions based on different scenarios. This capability helps organizations understand the potential risks and opportunities associated with changes in their operating environment.

Graphical Representation and Data Visualization:

Spreadsheet software allows organizations to create visually appealing charts and graphs to represent budgeted amounts and variances. These visual representations facilitate the understanding of financial information and make it easier to communicate budget, related insights to stakeholders. Organizations can use bar charts, line graphs, or pie charts to illustrate the composition of expenses, revenue trends, or variances between actual results and the flexible budget. Graphical representation enhances data visualization, making it easier to identify patterns, trends, and outliers within the budget data.

Collaboration and Version Control:

Spreadsheet software supports collaboration among multiple users, allowing teams to work together on developing and reviewing flexible budgets. Organizations can share spreadsheets with relevant stakeholders, granting them access to make edits or comments. The software provides features for tracking changes, facilitating version control, and ensuring that all contributors work on the most up, to, date version of the budget. Collaboration and version control capabilities streamline the budgeting process, promote transparency, and foster collective decision, making.

Flexibility and Adaptability:

As the name suggests, spreadsheet software provides the flexibility required for flexible budgeting. Organizations can easily modify budgeted amounts by adjusting the formulas or input values in the spreadsheet. This adaptability allows organizations to update budgeted amounts based on actual performance, changes in activity levels, or new information. Spreadsheet software empowers organizations to respond quickly to changing circumstances, facilitating dynamic financial planning and enhancing the accuracy and relevance of the flexible budget.

Advanced Budgeting Software Options

Embracing the Future: Exploring Advanced Budgeting Software Options

Budgeting plays a critical role in the financial management of organizations. With the advancements in technology, budgeting software has evolved significantly, offering advanced features and capabilities that enhance the efficiency, accuracy, and effectiveness of budgeting processes. In the context of flexible budgeting, organizations can leverage advanced budgeting software options to streamline their financial planning, analysis, and decision, making. Below we will explore some of the advanced budgeting software options available, highlighting their benefits and applications in relation to flexible budgeting.

Cloud, Based Budgeting Software:

Cloud, based budgeting software provides organizations with the flexibility to access and manage budgeting data from anywhere, at any time. These software options store budgeting data in the cloud, eliminating the need for on, premises infrastructure and enabling real, time collaboration among users. With cloud, based software, organizations can easily share budgeting information with stakeholders, facilitate remote collaboration, and ensure that all users have access to the most up, to, date budgeting data. This accessibility and collaboration foster seamless flexible budgeting processes and support dynamic decision, making.

Integrated Financial Management Systems:

Integrated financial management systems offer comprehensive solutions that encompass budgeting, forecasting, accounting, and performance management. These software options provide a centralized platform for managing financial information, ensuring seamless integration between different financial processes. By integrating budgeting with other financial functions, organizations can align budgeted amounts with strategic objectives, track actual performance, and conduct real, time analysis. Integrated financial management systems promote accurate and efficient flexible budgeting by eliminating data silos and enhancing data consistency across various financial processes.

Data Visualization Tools:

Data visualization tools are designed to transform complex budgeting data into visual representations such as charts, graphs, and dashboards. These tools enable organizations to gain insights from budgeting data quickly and effectively. By visualizing budgeted amounts, variances, and trends, organizations can identify patterns, outliers, and opportunities within the data. Data visualization tools enhance the understanding and communication of budgeting information, enabling stakeholders to make informed decisions based on clear and intuitive representations of financial data. This visual approach supports effective flexible budgeting by facilitating data analysis and promoting data, driven decision, making.

Advanced Forecasting and Predictive Analytics:

Advanced budgeting software options incorporate forecasting and predictive analytics capabilities, enabling organizations to make more accurate predictions and projections. These software options leverage historical data, statistical models, and machine learning algorithms to generate forecasts and predict future financial outcomes. By incorporating advanced forecasting techniques, organizations can better anticipate changes in activity levels, market conditions, or resource requirements, allowing for more accurate and reliable flexible budgets. The integration of predictive analytics enhances the ability to identify trends, patterns, and potential risks, supporting proactive decision, making and strategic planning.

Automation and Workflow Management:

Advanced budgeting software options offer automation features and workflow management capabilities that streamline the budgeting process. These features automate repetitive tasks, such as data entry, consolidation, and calculations, saving time and reducing the risk of manual errors. Workflow management tools enable organizations to define and track the progress of budgeting activities, ensuring that the budgeting process follows a structured and timely approach. Automation and workflow management features enhance the efficiency of flexible budgeting, freeing up resources for more value, added activities and improving overall productivity.

Advanced Scenario Planning and What, If Analysis:

Advanced budgeting software options provide robust scenario planning and what, if analysis functionalities. Organizations can create multiple scenarios based on different assumptions, variables, and events to evaluate the financial impact of various conditions or decisions. These software options enable organizations to test different scenarios, adjust input parameters, and assess the resulting budgeted amounts and financial outcomes.

The Impact of Automation on Budgeting

Revolutionizing Financial Management: The Impact of Automation on Budgeting

Budgeting is a critical process that allows organizations to plan, allocate, and control their financial resources effectively. In recent years, automation has emerged as a game, changer in various industries, transforming traditional practices and revolutionizing business operations. The impact of automation on budgeting has been particularly significant, offering numerous benefits in terms of efficiency, accuracy, and adaptability. Below we will explore the impact of automation on budgeting, specifically in relation to flexible budgeting, and delve into the advantages and implications of this technological advancement.

Streamlined Data Collection and Entry:

Automation streamlines the data collection and entry process in budgeting. With the integration of accounting systems and financial software, organizations can automate the retrieval and consolidation of financial data, reducing the reliance on manual input. This not only saves time but also minimizes the risk of human errors. By eliminating tedious and repetitive tasks, automation frees up valuable resources that can be redirected towards higher, value activities, such as data analysis and strategic decision, making.

Enhanced Accuracy and Consistency:

Automation significantly improves the accuracy and consistency of budgeting processes. Manual data entry is prone to errors, such as typos or miscalculations, which can have a cascading effect on the entire budgeting process. By automating data collection and calculations, organizations can eliminate these errors and ensure data integrity. Automation also enforces consistency in budgeting practices by applying predefined rules and formulas consistently across the entire budgeting process. This standardized approach enhances the reliability of budgeted amounts and improves the overall quality of financial planning.

Real, Time Data Analysis and Reporting:

Automation enables real, time data analysis and reporting, providing organizations with up, to, date insights into their financial performance. With automated systems, organizations can generate reports and analyze data on, demand, rather than relying on manually compiled reports that may be outdated by the time they are reviewed. Real, time data analysis enables organizations to identify trends, patterns, and anomalies promptly. This agility allows for proactive decision, making, facilitating timely adjustments to the flexible budget based on the latest information.

Improved Flexibility and Adaptability:

Flexible budgeting requires organizations to adjust their budgeted amounts based on changing circumstances. Automation enhances the flexibility and adaptability of budgeting processes by enabling dynamic updates to budgeted amounts. Organizations can easily modify and recalculate budget figures as new information becomes available, such as changes in activity levels, market conditions, or resource availability. This flexibility ensures that the flexible budget remains relevant and aligned with the organization's evolving needs and goals.

Efficient Scenario Planning and What, If Analysis:

Automation simplifies scenario planning and what, if analysis in budgeting. Organizations can create multiple scenarios with different assumptions and variables to assess the financial impact of various situations. Automation allows for the swift generation of budgeted amounts under different scenarios, eliminating the need for manual recalculations. This capability enables organizations to evaluate the potential outcomes of different strategies, make informed decisions, and develop contingency plans accordingly. Efficient scenario planning and what, if analysis enhance the organization's ability to anticipate risks, seize opportunities, and adapt to changing market dynamics.

Enhanced Collaboration and Communication:

Automation facilitates collaboration and communication among stakeholders involved in the budgeting process. Cloud, based budgeting software and shared online platforms allow multiple users to access and work on the budget simultaneously, regardless of their physical location. This collaborative approach fosters efficient information exchange, encourages stakeholder engagement, and reduces communication gaps. By automating the budgeting process, organizations can achieve greater transparency, accountability, and collaboration, ultimately improving the quality and acceptance of the flexible budget.

Chapter Ten

Future Trends in Flexible Budgeting

Paving the Way: Future Trends in Flexible Budgeting

Flexible budgeting has become an integral part of financial management, empowering organizations to adapt to dynamic business environments and optimize resource allocation. As technology continues to advance and market conditions evolve, the landscape of flexible budgeting is poised for transformation. Below we will explore the future trends in flexible budgeting, examining how emerging technologies, changing business models, and evolving market dynamics are shaping the way organizations approach budgeting processes. By staying abreast of these trends, organizations can embrace the future of flexible budgeting and achieve greater financial agility.

Artificial Intelligence and Machine Learning:

Artificial intelligence (AI) and machine learning (ML) are poised to revolutionize the field of flexible budgeting. These technologies offer capabilities such as predictive analytics, pattern recognition, and natural language processing, which can enhance the accuracy and efficiency of budgeting processes. AI and ML algorithms can analyze large volumes of historical data, identify trends, and generate accurate forecasts for future activity levels or financial outcomes. By leveraging AI and ML, organizations can make data, driven decisions, improve the accuracy of budgeted amounts, and better anticipate changes in resource requirements.

Blockchain Technology:

Blockchain technology, known for its decentralized and secure nature, has the potential to transform the way budgeting processes are executed. With blockchain, organizations can create transparent and tamper, proof budgeting records, ensuring the integrity and traceability of budgeted amounts. Smart contracts, powered by blockchain, can automate budgeting processes and enforce predefined rules and workflows. This technology enhances trust, reduces the risk of fraud, and simplifies the reconciliation of budgeted amounts across multiple stakeholders. By leveraging blockchain technology, organizations can enhance the efficiency, transparency, and accountability of flexible budgeting.

Real, Time Data Integration:

Real, time data integration is becoming increasingly crucial for organizations as they strive to make informed and timely budgeting decisions. With advancements in data integration technologies, organizations can seamlessly integrate data from various sources, including external market data, customer insights, and operational metrics. Real, time data integration enables organizations to monitor changes in activity levels, market conditions, or resource availability and adjust budgeted amounts accordingly. By leveraging real, time data integration, organizations can ensure that their flexible budgets reflect the most up, to, date information, enabling agile decision, making and resource allocation.

Dynamic Forecasting Models:

Traditional budgeting processes often rely on static forecasting models that may not capture the complexities and uncertainties of business environments. Future trends in flexible budgeting will see the emergence of dynamic forecasting models that can adapt to changing circumstances in real, time. These models incorporate external factors, such as market trends, competitor analysis, and economic indicators, to generate more accurate and responsive forecasts. Dynamic forecasting models empower organizations to proactively adjust budgeted amounts, anticipate risks, and capitalize on opportunities, enhancing the effectiveness of flexible budgeting in a rapidly changing landscape.

Integrated Performance Management:

Future trends in flexible budgeting emphasize the integration of budgeting with performance management processes. Organizations are recognizing the need for a holistic view of financial performance, which goes beyond traditional budget, versus, actual analysis. Integrated performance management systems enable organizations to track performance against strategic objectives, key performance indicators (KPIs), and benchmarks. By integrating budgeting with performance management, organizations can align budgeted amounts with performance targets, track progress in real, time, and evaluate the impact of budget adjustments on financial outcomes. Integrated performance management enhances accountability, transparency, and informed decision, making in flexible budgeting.

Scenario, Based Planning:

As business environments become increasingly uncertain and volatile, scenario, based planning will play a crucial role in flexible budgeting. Future trends in flexible budgeting will see organizations developing multiple scenarios based on different assumptions and external factors.

The Increasing Importance of Agility in Budgeting

Embracing Change: The Increasing Importance of Agility in Budgeting

Budgeting has long been considered a crucial process for organizations to plan, allocate resources, and monitor financial performance. However, in today's rapidly changing business landscape, traditional budgeting practices often fall short in addressing the dynamic nature of markets, customer demands, and technological advancements. As a result, the importance of agility in budgeting has significantly increased. Organizations are recognizing the need for flexible budgeting approaches that can adapt to changing circumstances and enable proactive decision, making. Below we will explore the increasing importance of agility in budgeting, specifically in relation to flexible budgeting, and discuss how organizations can embrace this shift to enhance their financial management practices.

Changing Business Environment:

The business environment is evolving at an unprecedented pace, driven by technological advancements, globalization, and shifting consumer preferences. Organizations are faced with unpredictable market conditions, disruptive innovations, and regulatory changes. Traditional budgeting processes that rely on static assumptions and inflexible plans may hinder organizations' ability to respond effectively to these changes. Agile budgeting practices, such as flexible budgeting, allow organizations to adjust budgeted amounts based on emerging trends, market fluctuations, and customer demands. This agility enables organizations to seize opportunities and mitigate risks in a rapidly changing landscape.

Enhanced Decision, Making:

Agility in budgeting promotes enhanced decision, making capabilities. Traditional budgeting processes often involve rigid plans and fixed allocations that limit organizations' ability to adapt to unforeseen circumstances. Agile budgeting practices, on the other hand, encourage a proactive approach to decision, making by allowing organizations to adjust budgeted amounts based on real, time information and changing business conditions. This flexibility enables organizations to make timely decisions, allocate resources strategically, and seize opportunities as they arise. The ability to respond quickly and effectively to market dynamics is a significant advantage in today's competitive landscape.

Improved Resource Allocation:

Agility in budgeting facilitates improved resource allocation by aligning budgeted amounts with organizational priorities and performance targets. Traditional budgeting practices often allocate resources based on historical data or incremental changes, without considering the strategic goals and changing business needs. Agile budgeting, such as flexible budgeting, enables organizations to allocate resources based on the achieved activity levels or changes in business operations. This approach ensures that resources are deployed efficiently and effectively to areas that generate the most value and contribute to organizational objectives. By optimizing resource allocation, organizations can enhance productivity, reduce waste, and achieve better financial outcomes.

Enhanced Risk Management:

Agility in budgeting plays a crucial role in enhancing risk management capabilities. The business landscape is fraught with uncertainties, including economic volatility, regulatory changes, and geopolitical risks. Traditional budgeting processes may not adequately address these risks, as they are often based on fixed assumptions and limited scenarios. Agile budgeting practices allow organizations to incorporate risk factors into budgeting decisions, conduct scenario, based planning, and assess the financial implications of different risk scenarios. This proactive approach to risk management enables organizations to identify potential threats, develop contingency plans, and mitigate the impact of adverse events on financial performance.

Customer, Centric Approach:

Agility in budgeting aligns with a customer, centric approach, placing the customer at the center of budgeting decisions. Today's customers are more empowered and demanding than ever, with changing preferences and evolving expectations. Traditional budgeting processes may overlook the importance of customer, centricity, leading to misalignment between budgeted amounts and customer needs. Agile budgeting practices emphasize the importance of customer insights, market trends, and customer, driven metrics in budgeting decisions. By adopting a customer, centric approach, organizations can allocate resources effectively to initiatives that drive customer satisfaction, loyalty, and long, term profitability.

The Role of Big Data and Analytics in Budgeting

Unleashing the Power: The Role of Big Data and Analytics in Budgeting

Budgeting is a critical process for organizations to allocate resources, plan operations, and monitor financial performance. In recent years, the proliferation of data and advancements in analytics technologies have opened new possibilities in budgeting practices. Big data and analytics have emerged as game, changers, providing organizations with the ability to leverage vast amounts of information and gain valuable insights. Below we will explore the role of big data and analytics in budgeting, with a specific focus on flexible budgeting. We will examine how organizations can harness the power of data and analytics to enhance their budgeting processes, improve decision, making, and drive financial success.

Data, Driven Decision Making:

Big data and analytics empower organizations to make data, driven decisions in budgeting. Traditionally, budgeting decisions relied heavily on historical data and assumptions. However, with the advent of big data, organizations can now access a wealth of structured and unstructured data from various sources, including customer interactions, market trends, and operational metrics. By harnessing this data and applying advanced analytics techniques, organizations can gain valuable insights into customer behavior, market dynamics, and business operations. These insights enable more informed budgeting decisions, allowing organizations to allocate resources effectively based on data, backed evidence.

Improved Accuracy and Granularity:

The availability of big data and analytics enables organizations to achieve greater accuracy and granularity in budgeting. Traditional budgeting processes often relied on aggregated data or assumptions, which may overlook the nuances and complexities of business operations. With big data and analytics, organizations can analyze data at a more granular level, such as customer segments, product lines, or geographic regions. This detailed analysis provides a more accurate understanding of cost drivers, revenue streams, and resource requirements. By incorporating granular insights into the budgeting process, organizations can optimize their budgeted amounts, allocate resources strategically, and achieve better financial outcomes.

Enhanced Forecasting and Predictive Capabilities:

Big data and analytics enhance organizations' forecasting and predictive capabilities in budgeting. Traditional budgeting processes often relied on historical trends and linear projections, which may not capture the complexities and uncertainties of the business environment. With big data and analytics, organizations can leverage advanced forecasting models, machine learning algorithms, and predictive analytics to generate more accurate and robust forecasts. These techniques analyze historical data, identify patterns, and detect trends to make predictions about future financial outcomes. By incorporating advanced forecasting and predictive capabilities into budgeting, organizations can anticipate changes, adapt their budgeted amounts, and make more informed decisions based on future projections.

Real, Time Data Analysis and Monitoring:

Big data and analytics enable real, time data analysis and monitoring in budgeting. Traditional budgeting processes often relied on periodic reporting and static data snapshots, which limited organizations' ability to respond quickly to changes. With big data and analytics, organizations can access and analyze data in real, time, allowing for dynamic monitoring of financial performance, key performance indicators (KPIs), and budget variances. Real, time data analysis enables organizations to identify issues, detect anomalies, and make timely adjustments to their budgeted amounts. By adopting a real, time approach, organizations can enhance their responsiveness, optimize resource allocation, and ensure that their flexible budgets reflect the most current information.

Scenario Planning and What, If Analysis:

Big data and analytics facilitate scenario planning and what, if analysis in budgeting. Organizations face uncertainties and risks in the business environment, such as market fluctuations, regulatory changes, or competitive disruptions. Traditional budgeting processes often struggled to incorporate these factors effectively. With big data and analytics, organizations can simulate different scenarios and conduct what, if analysis to assess the financial impact of various conditions or decisions.

The Impact of Economic Changes on Flexible Budgeting

Navigating the Tides: The Impact of Economic Changes on Flexible Budgeting

Flexible budgeting is a dynamic financial management approach that enables organizations to adapt to changing circumstances and optimize resource allocation. However, the effectiveness of flexible budgeting is greatly influenced by economic changes. Economic conditions, such as inflation, recession, or changes in market demand, can have a significant impact on budgeted amounts and financial outcomes. Below we will explore the impact of economic changes on flexible budgeting and discuss how organizations can navigate these challenges to maintain financial stability and success.

Inflation and Price Fluctuations:

Inflation is an economic phenomenon characterized by a sustained increase in the general price level of goods and services. Inflationary periods can have a profound impact on flexible budgeting. Rising prices can increase the cost of inputs, such as raw materials or labor, which may lead to higher budgeted amounts for expenses. Flexible budgeting allows organizations to adjust budgeted amounts based on the prevailing economic conditions, enabling them to account for inflationary pressures and maintain profitability. By regularly reviewing and revising budgeted amounts in response to inflation, organizations can effectively manage their cost structures and ensure financial viability.

Economic Recession and Contraction:

Economic recessions and contractions pose significant challenges to organizations' budgeting processes. During economic downturns, consumer demand often declines, leading to reduced sales and revenue streams. This can have a direct impact on budgeted amounts for sales and overall revenue projections. In such scenarios, flexible budgeting becomes crucial for organizations to align their expenses with the reduced revenue expectations. By adjusting budgeted amounts for expenses such as marketing, production, and overhead costs, organizations can mitigate the impact of economic contractions and maintain financial stability.

Changing Market Dynamics:

Flexible budgeting is particularly important when organizations face changing market dynamics. Markets are constantly evolving, driven by factors such as technological advancements, shifting consumer preferences, and emerging competitors. These changes can disrupt existing business models and require organizations to adapt their budgeted amounts accordingly. Flexible budgeting allows organizations to reallocate resources to new growth areas, invest in innovative initiatives, and capitalize on emerging market opportunities. By embracing a flexible approach, organizations can align their budgeted amounts with changing market dynamics and remain competitive in the face of economic shifts.

Fluctuating Exchange Rates:

Fluctuations in exchange rates can significantly impact organizations' budgeting processes, particularly for those operating in global markets. Currency fluctuations can affect the cost of imports, exports, and international transactions, leading to changes in budgeted amounts for expenses and revenue projections. Flexible budgeting enables organizations to monitor exchange rate fluctuations and adjust budgeted amounts accordingly. By factoring in the impact of exchange rate changes, organizations can ensure that their budgeted amounts reflect the economic reality of international operations and mitigate potential risks associated with currency fluctuations.

Regulatory Changes:

Economic changes often go hand in hand with regulatory changes. Governments may introduce new policies, tax reforms, or industry, specific regulations that impact organizations' budgeting processes. Flexible budgeting allows organizations to adapt their budgeted amounts to comply with regulatory requirements and incorporate the financial impact of new regulations. By monitoring changes in the regulatory landscape and adjusting budgeted amounts in response, organizations can ensure compliance, manage potential risks, and maintain financial stability in the face of evolving economic and regulatory environments.

Technological Advancements:

Technological advancements have a profound impact on the economy, industries, and organizations' budgeting processes. The emergence of new technologies can disrupt existing business models, create new revenue streams, and influence budgeted amounts for expenses.

Chapter Eleven

Overcoming Challenges in Flexible Budgeting

Embracing Resilience: Overcoming Challenges in Flexible Budgeting

Flexible budgeting is a dynamic approach that enables organizations to adapt to changing circumstances and optimize resource allocation. While flexible budgeting offers numerous benefits, it is not without its challenges. Organizations may encounter obstacles that impede the successful implementation and execution of flexible budgeting practices. These challenges may include resistance to change, data accuracy issues, and the complexity of adjusting budgeted amounts. Below we will explore key challenges in flexible budgeting and discuss strategies to overcome them, ensuring the effective utilization of flexible budgeting as a financial management tool.

Resistance to Change:

One of the significant challenges organizations face when implementing flexible budgeting is resistance to change. People are often accustomed to traditional budgeting methods and may resist adopting a more dynamic approach. To overcome this challenge, organizations need to emphasize the benefits of flexible budgeting, such as improved decision, making, better resource allocation, and enhanced adaptability. Clear communication, training programs, and engaging stakeholders in the process can help alleviate resistance and build support for flexible budgeting.

Data Accuracy and Availability:

Accurate and reliable data is critical for effective flexible budgeting. However, organizations may face challenges in obtaining accurate data in a timely manner. Data may be scattered across different systems, departments, or formats, making it difficult to consolidate and analyze. To address this challenge, organizations should invest in robust data management systems and processes. By centralizing data sources, implementing data quality controls, and establishing data governance frameworks, organizations can ensure the accuracy and availability of data for flexible budgeting purposes.

Complexity of Adjusting Budgeted Amounts:

Adjusting budgeted amounts can be complex, especially in organizations with multiple departments or business units. Ensuring that budgeted amounts are aligned with changing circumstances requires collaboration and coordination among various stakeholders. Organizations should establish clear processes for reviewing and adjusting budgeted amounts. Regular communication and engagement with department heads or budget owners can facilitate a smooth adjustment process. By involving key stakeholders in the budgeting process, organizations can address the complexity of adjusting budgeted amounts and ensure alignment with organizational goals.

Balancing Flexibility and Control:

Flexible budgeting introduces a level of uncertainty and flexibility that may challenge organizations' desire for control. Some stakeholders may express concerns about potential budget variances and the perceived loss of control over spending. To address this challenge, organizations should establish clear guidelines and control mechanisms within the flexible budgeting framework. Setting performance targets, monitoring variances, and implementing regular review processes can provide a balance between flexibility and control. By ensuring accountability and transparency, organizations can maintain control while benefiting from the flexibility of budgeting.

Integration with Strategic Planning:

Flexible budgeting needs to align with the organization's strategic planning process to be effective. However, organizations may face challenges in integrating the two processes seamlessly. To overcome this challenge, organizations should promote collaboration between the budgeting and strategic planning teams. Regular communication and shared objectives can ensure that budgeted amounts reflect the strategic goals and priorities of the organization. By aligning the budgeting process with strategic planning, organizations can overcome challenges and achieve a cohesive approach to financial management.

Continuous Monitoring and Evaluation:

An ongoing challenge in flexible budgeting is the need for continuous monitoring and evaluation. As circumstances change, organizations must continually assess and adjust budgeted amounts to remain responsive and agile. This requires regular review processes, monitoring of key performance indicators, and proactive communication among stakeholders. By establishing a framework for continuous monitoring and evaluation, organizations can address challenges and identify areas for improvement in the flexible budgeting process. Regular performance assessments help organizations stay on track, make informed decisions, and adapt to changing conditions effectively.

Identifying Common Budgeting Mistakes

Navigating the Path to Success: Identifying Common Budgeting Mistakes

Budgeting is a fundamental process that organizations use to plan, allocate resources, and monitor financial performance. While budgeting provides valuable insights and guidance, it is not immune to mistakes and challenges. Understanding and identifying common budgeting mistakes is essential for organizations to optimize their financial management practices and achieve their goals. In the context of flexible budgeting, avoiding these mistakes becomes even more critical. Below we will explore some common budgeting mistakes and discuss strategies to address them, ensuring the effectiveness of flexible budgeting and driving financial success.

Unrealistic Revenue Projections:

One common budgeting mistake is setting unrealistic revenue projections. Organizations may be overly optimistic in estimating future revenues, leading to inflated expectations and unreliable budgeting figures. To address this mistake, organizations should conduct thorough market research, analyze historical data, and consider external factors that may impact revenue generation. By adopting a realistic approach to revenue projections, organizations can establish more accurate budgets that align with the actual potential of the business.

Neglecting Variable and Controllable Costs:

Another mistake is neglecting variable and controllable costs in the budgeting process. Organizations often focus on fixed costs and overlook variable costs that can be influenced or managed. Flexible budgeting requires organizations to consider both fixed and variable costs to accurately reflect the changing nature of business operations. By analyzing variable costs, organizations can identify areas for cost optimization, prioritize spending, and allocate resources effectively. Neglecting variable costs can lead to inaccurate budgeting figures and missed opportunities for cost savings.

Failure to Account for Seasonality:

Many organizations overlook seasonality when budgeting, leading to inaccurate financial plans. Seasonal variations can significantly impact revenue and expenses in certain industries or periods. Ignoring these fluctuations can result in budget variances and financial instability. To address this mistake, organizations should conduct thorough analysis of historical data, identify seasonal trends, and adjust budgeted amounts accordingly. By incorporating seasonality into the budgeting process, organizations can improve accuracy and better anticipate financial challenges during specific periods.

Inadequate Communication and Collaboration:

Poor communication and collaboration among stakeholders can undermine the effectiveness of budgeting. When departments or individuals work in isolation, it can lead to misalignment, duplication of efforts, and inaccurate budgeting figures. To overcome this mistake, organizations should foster a culture of collaboration, establish clear communication channels, and involve relevant stakeholders in the budgeting process. By encouraging open dialogue, sharing information, and collaborating on budgeting decisions, organizations can ensure that budgets reflect a holistic understanding of the business and promote buy, in from key stakeholders.

Overlooking Contingency Planning:

Failure to incorporate contingency planning is a significant budgeting mistake. Uncertainties and unforeseen events can impact financial performance, and organizations must be prepared to address them. A flexible budgeting approach necessitates the inclusion of contingency plans to mitigate risks and respond to unexpected circumstances. By allocating resources for unforeseen expenses, organizations can proactively manage risks and maintain financial stability. Overlooking contingency planning leaves organizations vulnerable to financial setbacks and hinders their ability to adapt to changing conditions.

Lack of Regular Monitoring and Review:

A common mistake in budgeting is the lack of regular monitoring and review of budgeted amounts. Budgets should not be set in stone but rather treated as dynamic tools that require continuous evaluation and adjustment. Organizations that fail to monitor and review their budgets regularly may miss out on opportunities for improvement, fail to address variances, and lose the ability to adapt to changing circumstances. To avoid this mistake, organizations should establish regular review cycles, track actual performance against budgeted amounts, and implement timely adjustments when necessary. Regular monitoring and review enable organizations to stay proactive, identify potential issues, and optimize resource allocation for better financial outcomes.

How to Mitigate Risks in Flexible Budgeting

Navigating the Waters: How to Mitigate Risks in Flexible Budgeting

Flexible budgeting offers organizations the ability to adapt to changing circumstances, optimize resource allocation, and drive financial success. However, like any financial management approach, flexible budgeting comes with its own set of risks. Understanding and mitigating these risks is essential for organizations to fully harness the benefits of flexible budgeting and ensure its effectiveness. Below we will explore strategies to mitigate risks in flexible budgeting, enabling organizations to navigate uncertainties and achieve their financial objectives.

Establish Realistic Assumptions and Scenarios:

A key step in mitigating risks in flexible budgeting is to establish realistic assumptions and scenarios. Uncertainties and unexpected events can impact financial performance, and organizations must consider various scenarios during the budgeting process. By conducting sensitivity analysis and stress testing, organizations can evaluate the potential impact of different factors on budgeted amounts. This enables them to establish more realistic assumptions, identify potential risks, and develop contingency plans to address them.

Incorporate Risk Management Practices:

Risk management is essential for mitigating risks in flexible budgeting. Organizations should implement robust risk management practices and frameworks to identify, assess, and mitigate risks. This involves identifying potential risks, evaluating their likelihood and impact, and developing risk mitigation strategies. By integrating risk management into the budgeting process, organizations can proactively address risks and respond effectively to unexpected events. Regular risk assessments and mitigation activities ensure that potential risks are identified and managed throughout the budgeting cycle.

Foster Collaboration and Communication:

Collaboration and communication are critical in mitigating risks in flexible budgeting. When stakeholders work in silos or lack effective communication channels, it hinders the organization's ability to identify and address risks in a timely manner. To mitigate this risk, organizations should foster a culture of collaboration and establish clear communication channels across departments and functions. By involving key stakeholders in the budgeting process, organizations can leverage diverse perspectives, share insights, and collectively identify and address potential risks.

Implement Monitoring and Control Mechanisms:

Monitoring and control mechanisms play a vital role in mitigating risks in flexible budgeting. Organizations should establish robust monitoring processes to track actual performance against budgeted amounts. This includes regular review of financial data, variance analysis, and performance metrics. By implementing control mechanisms, organizations can identify deviations from the budget, investigate the underlying causes, and take corrective actions. Monitoring and control provide early warning signals, enabling organizations to mitigate risks and make informed decisions for optimal resource allocation.

Embrace Technology and Automation:

Leveraging technology and automation can significantly enhance risk mitigation in flexible budgeting. Budgeting software, advanced analytics tools, and data visualization platforms can streamline the budgeting process, improve accuracy, and facilitate real, time monitoring. By automating routine tasks, organizations can reduce the risk of human error and enhance the efficiency of budgeting activities. Furthermore, technology enables organizations to access real, time data, analyze trends, and identify potential risks promptly. Embracing technology empowers organizations to make informed decisions and mitigate risks effectively.

Develop Contingency Plans:

Developing contingency plans is crucial for mitigating risks in flexible budgeting. Organizations should anticipate potential risks and develop predefined response plans to address them. Contingency plans outline specific actions to be taken in response to various risks, allowing organizations to respond quickly and effectively when faced with unexpected events. These plans should include alternative resource allocation strategies, cost reduction measures, and revised revenue projections. By developing and periodically reviewing contingency plans, organizations can minimize the impact of risks on the budgeting process and financial performance.

Navigating Uncertainties in Revenue and Costs

Sailing Through Uncertainties: Navigating Uncertainties in Revenue and Costs with Flexible Budgeting

In the business world, uncertainties in revenue and costs are common challenges that organizations face. Fluctuations in market conditions, unexpected events, and evolving customer demands can impact both revenue generation and cost structures. To effectively manage these uncertainties, organizations can turn to flexible budgeting—a dynamic approach that allows for adjustments in response to changing circumstances. Below we will explore strategies to navigate uncertainties in revenue and costs with flexible budgeting, enabling organizations to optimize their financial management practices and drive success.

Conduct Thorough Market Research:

Thorough market research is essential to navigate uncertainties in revenue and costs. Organizations should continuously gather and analyze market data, monitor industry trends, and understand customer preferences. This enables them to make informed revenue projections and anticipate potential shifts in demand. By conducting market research, organizations can stay ahead of the curve, identify new revenue opportunities, and adapt their cost structures to align with changing market dynamics.

Incorporate Scenario Planning:

Scenario planning is a valuable tool for navigating uncertainties in revenue and costs. It involves developing multiple scenarios that reflect different possible outcomes based on varying market conditions. Organizations can create optimistic, pessimistic, and moderate scenarios to assess the potential impact on revenue and costs. By incorporating scenario planning into the budgeting process, organizations can prepare for different eventualities and develop contingency plans to mitigate risks.

Embrace Agile Decision, Making:

Agile decision, making is crucial in navigating uncertainties in revenue and costs. Organizations should adopt a flexible and responsive approach to decision, making, allowing them to adjust strategies and resource allocations quickly. By embracing agile decision, making, organizations can seize revenue opportunities, optimize cost structures, and adapt to changing market conditions. This approach enables organizations to make informed decisions based on real, time data and align their revenue and cost plans accordingly.

Implement Rolling Forecasts:

Rolling forecasts are an effective strategy for managing uncertainties in revenue and costs. Unlike traditional static budgets, rolling forecasts provide a continuous projection of future revenue and costs over a defined period. By updating forecasts regularly, organizations can adjust their revenue and cost expectations based on the most recent information available. Rolling forecasts enable organizations to respond promptly to changes, identify emerging trends, and make informed decisions to optimize financial performance.

Foster Collaboration and Communication:

Collaboration and communication are essential in navigating uncertainties in revenue and costs. Organizations should foster a culture that encourages cross, functional collaboration and open communication channels. By involving key stakeholders from various departments, organizations can gain diverse perspectives and insights. This collaborative approach facilitates the identification of revenue opportunities and cost, saving measures. Effective communication ensures that relevant information is shared promptly, enabling agile decision, making and alignment between revenue and cost plans.

Monitor Key Performance Indicators (KPIs):

Monitoring key performance indicators (KPIs) is vital for navigating uncertainties in revenue and costs. Organizations should identify and track relevant KPIs that reflect their revenue and cost drivers. By monitoring KPIs regularly, organizations can assess their financial performance, identify deviations from projections, and take corrective actions. This proactive approach helps organizations stay on track, detect potential issues early on, and make data, driven decisions to optimize revenue and control costs.

Embrace Continuous Improvement:

Continuous improvement is a fundamental principle in navigating uncertainties in revenue and costs. Organizations should foster a culture of learning and innovation, encouraging employees to seek process efficiencies, identify cost, saving opportunities, and explore new revenue streams. By embracing continuous improvement, organizations can adapt to market changes, optimize their cost structures, and identify new ways to generate revenue. This iterative approach allows organizations to navigate uncertainties effectively and stay ahead of the competition.

Chapter Twelve

Flexible Budgeting for Personal Finances

Flex Your Finances: Embracing Flexible Budgeting for Personal Financial Success

Budgeting is not just for businesses—it is equally essential for personal financial management. By implementing flexible budgeting practices, individuals can take control of their finances, achieve their goals, and navigate uncertainties effectively. Flexible budgeting for personal finances involves creating a dynamic budget that adapts to changes in income, expenses, and financial goals. Below we will explore the benefits of flexible budgeting for personal finances and discuss strategies to implement it successfully, empowering individuals to make informed financial decisions and attain long, term financial success.

Set Clear Financial Goals:

Setting clear financial goals is the foundation of successful budgeting. Before creating a flexible budget, individuals should identify their short, term and long, term financial objectives. These goals could include saving for emergencies, paying off debt, investing for retirement, or saving for a major purchase. By establishing clear goals, individuals can align their budgeting efforts and make informed decisions that support their financial aspirations.

Track Income and Expenses:

To effectively implement flexible budgeting, individuals must have a clear understanding of their income and expenses. Tracking income and expenses allows individuals to assess their financial situation accurately and identify areas where they can make adjustments. By categorizing expenses and monitoring income streams, individuals can identify patterns, track trends, and make informed decisions about their spending and saving habits.

Embrace Flexibility:

Flexibility is a core principle of flexible budgeting for personal finances. Life is dynamic, and circumstances may change unexpectedly. By embracing flexibility, individuals can adapt their budget to accommodate changes in income, expenses, or financial goals. This may include adjusting spending categories, reallocating resources, or revising savings targets. The ability to adapt to changes empowers individuals to stay on track and make financially sound decisions in the face of uncertainties.

Prioritize Saving and Investing:

Savings and investments are integral to personal financial success. Within a flexible budget, individuals should prioritize saving and investing by allocating a portion of their income to these goals. Whether it is building an emergency fund or contributing to retirement accounts, consistent saving and investing are key to long, term financial stability and growth. By prioritizing saving and investing in the budget, individuals can secure their financial future and take advantage of compounding returns over time.

Allocate for Variable Expenses:

Flexible budgeting acknowledges that not all expenses are fixed. Variable expenses, such as groceries, entertainment, or transportation, can fluctuate from month to month. Individuals should allocate a portion of their budget for these variable expenses, while still maintaining a reasonable spending limit. By monitoring and adjusting these categories regularly, individuals can manage their variable expenses effectively without compromising their overall financial health.

Plan for Financial Emergencies:

Financial emergencies can have a significant impact on personal finances. It is crucial to plan and budget for such unforeseen circumstances. Creating an emergency fund within a flexible budget ensures that individuals have a safety net to cover unexpected expenses, such as medical bills or car repairs. By consistently setting aside funds for emergencies, individuals can navigate financial setbacks without derailing their long, term financial goals.

Review and Adjust Regularly:

Regular review and adjustment are key to successful flexible budgeting for personal finances. Individuals should review their budget on a monthly or quarterly basis to assess progress, identify areas for improvement, and make necessary adjustments. This allows individuals to track their financial performance, evaluate their spending habits, and identify opportunities to optimize their budget. Regular review and adjustment ensure that individuals stay on track to achieve their financial goals.

Leverage Technology:

In the digital age, technology can be a valuable tool for personal budgeting. There are numerous budgeting apps and software available that can streamline the budgeting process, track expenses, and provide real, time financial insights.

Adapting Flexible Budgeting for Personal Use

Unleashing Financial Freedom: Adapting Flexible Budgeting for Personal Use

Flexible budgeting is not limited to businesses alone; it is an invaluable tool that individuals can use to take control of their personal finances. By adopting flexible budgeting practices, individuals can allocate resources effectively, track their expenses, and achieve their financial goals. Adapting flexible budgeting for personal use involves tailoring budgeting principles to suit individual needs and circumstances. Below we will explore the benefits of flexible budgeting for personal use and discuss strategies to adapt it successfully, empowering individuals to make informed financial decisions, reduce debt, and secure their financial future.

Determine Your Financial Goals:

The first step in adapting flexible budgeting for personal use is to determine your financial goals. Assess your short, term and long, term aspirations, such as paying off debt, saving for a down payment on a house, or establishing an emergency fund. Clearly defining your goals will provide a roadmap for budgeting and help you prioritize your spending and saving habits.

Track Your Income and Expenses:

To effectively implement flexible budgeting, it is crucial to track your income and expenses. Keep a record of your income sources and categorize your expenses, including fixed expenses like rent or mortgage payments, utilities, and transportation costs, as well as variable expenses like dining out, entertainment, and shopping. Tracking your income and expenses will help you understand your cash flow and identify areas where adjustments can be made.

Embrace Flexibility:

Flexibility is at the core of personal flexible budgeting. Life is full of unexpected events and changes, and your budget should be able to accommodate them. Embrace the concept of flexibility by allowing room for adjustments in your budget when necessary. This could include reallocating funds from one category to another or modifying your saving targets. By embracing flexibility, you can adapt to changing circumstances without derailing your financial progress.

Prioritize Saving and Debt Reduction:

Saving and debt reduction should be key priorities in your personal flexible budget. Allocate a portion of your income towards savings and debt repayment. Aim to build an emergency fund to cover unexpected expenses and focus on reducing high, interest debt. By making saving and debt reduction a priority, you establish a solid financial foundation and reduce financial stress.

Categorize and Allocate Expenses:

Categorizing and allocating expenses is an essential aspect of personal flexible budgeting. Divide your expenses into categories such as housing, transportation, groceries, entertainment, and healthcare. Allocate a predetermined amount to each category based on your financial goals and priorities. This will provide structure to your spending and ensure that you allocate resources according to your priorities.

Review and Adjust Regularly:

Regular review and adjustment are critical in personal flexible budgeting. Set aside time each month or quarter to review your budget and assess your progress. Analyze your spending patterns, evaluate your progress towards your financial goals, and identify areas for improvement. Make necessary adjustments to your budget to optimize your financial management and ensure alignment with your objectives.

Be Mindful of Variable Expenses:

Variable expenses can significantly impact your budget. Be mindful of these expenses and find ways to manage them effectively. Look for opportunities to reduce costs without sacrificing quality. For example, consider meal planning, buying in bulk, or exploring cost, effective entertainment options. By managing variable expenses prudently, you can maintain control over your budget and allocate more resources towards your financial goals.

Seek Financial Education and Support:

Adapting flexible budgeting for personal use may require financial education and support. Educate yourself about personal finance concepts, investment options, and debt management strategies. Attend workshops, read books, or seek guidance from financial advisors. Additionally, consider connecting with like, minded individuals who can provide support and accountability in your financial journey.

Managing Personal Expenses with a Flexible Budget

Mastering Your Finances: Managing Personal Expenses with a Flexible Budget

Managing personal expenses is a critical aspect of maintaining financial well, being and achieving long, term financial goals. One effective approach to personal expense management is through the use of a flexible budget. By adopting flexible budgeting principles, individuals can gain control over their spending habits, make informed financial decisions, and allocate resources more effectively. Below we will explore the benefits of managing personal expenses with a flexible budget and discuss strategies to implement it successfully, empowering individuals to achieve financial stability and pursue their aspirations.

Assess Your Income and Fixed Expenses:

The first step in managing personal expenses with a flexible budget is to assess your income and fixed expenses. Calculate your total income from all sources and identify your fixed expenses, such as rent or mortgage payments, utility bills, insurance premiums, and loan repayments. Understanding your fixed expenses provides a foundation for allocating resources and ensures that essential financial obligations are met.

Track Your Variable Expenses:

Variable expenses play a significant role in personal budgeting. These expenses can vary from month to month and include categories such as groceries, dining out, entertainment, transportation, and discretionary spending. Tracking your variable expenses is essential for identifying spending patterns and making informed decisions to align your expenses with your financial goals.

Categorize and Prioritize Your Expenses:

Categorizing and prioritizing your expenses is a key component of managing personal expenses with a flexible budget. Divide your expenses into categories such as housing, transportation, food, healthcare, entertainment, and savings. Assign each category a priority level based on your financial goals and allocate resources accordingly. This approach ensures that you allocate resources in line with your priorities and prevents overspending in discretionary areas.

Set Realistic Spending Targets:

To effectively manage personal expenses, it is crucial to set realistic spending targets for each expense category. Consider your income, financial obligations, and desired savings goals when determining these targets. Be mindful of striking a balance between enjoying your present lifestyle and saving for future financial security. Setting realistic spending targets helps you stay on track and manage your expenses more effectively.

Embrace Flexibility and Adaptability:

One of the primary advantages of a flexible budget is the ability to embrace flexibility and adaptability. Life is full of unexpected events and changing circumstances. Your budget should be designed to accommodate such changes without derailing your financial progress. Embrace the concept of flexibility and be prepared to make adjustments when necessary. This could involve reallocating funds from one category to another or adjusting spending targets to align with new priorities.

Practice Conscious Spending:

Conscious spending is an essential mindset to adopt when managing personal expenses. Before making a purchase, ask yourself if it aligns with your financial goals and priorities. Consider whether the expense is a need or a want and evaluate its long, term value. Practicing conscious spending helps you avoid impulsive purchases and make intentional financial decisions that support your overall financial well, being.

Review and Adjust Regularly:

Regular review and adjustment are critical in managing personal expenses with a flexible budget. Schedule regular check, ins to review your budget, track your expenses, and assess your progress. Evaluate whether you are adhering to your spending targets and if any adjustments are necessary.

Regular reviews empower you to identify areas for improvement, make necessary adjustments, and optimize your spending habits.

Seek Cost, Saving Opportunities:

Managing personal expenses also involves seeking cost, saving opportunities. Look for ways to reduce costs without compromising on quality. Compare prices, search for discounts and deals, and consider alternative options. Explore cost, saving measures in areas such as groceries, transportation, utilities, and entertainment. Small adjustments in your spending habits can lead to significant savings over time.

Savings and Investments: A Flexible Approach

Adapting to Financial Growth: A Flexible Approach to Savings and Investments

Savings and investments are crucial components of financial growth and long, term wealth accumulation. However, the traditional approach of setting fixed savings targets and adhering to rigid investment strategies may not always align with changing financial circumstances and goals. Adopting a flexible approach to savings and investments allows individuals to adapt to evolving financial needs, seize opportunities, and optimize their wealth, building strategies. Below we will explore the benefits of a flexible approach to savings and investments and discuss strategies to implement it effectively, empowering individuals to achieve their financial objectives and build a secure future.

Evaluate Your Financial Goals:

Before adopting a flexible approach to savings and investments, it is essential to evaluate your financial goals. Consider your short, term and long, term objectives, such as creating an emergency fund, saving for a down payment on a house, planning for retirement, or funding education expenses. By understanding your financial goals, you can align your savings and investment strategies accordingly.

Set a Foundation with Fixed Savings:

While flexibility is key, establishing a foundation with fixed savings is a prudent starting point. Determine a fixed amount or percentage of your income to save consistently. This ensures that you build a financial cushion and develop a savings habit. Fixed savings provide stability and create a baseline for your flexible savings and investment approach.

Build an Emergency Fund:

An emergency fund is a crucial aspect of financial preparedness. It provides a safety net during unexpected events or financial setbacks. Allocate a portion of your savings towards building an emergency fund that covers several months' worth of living expenses. This fund should be readily accessible, preferably in a high, yield savings account, to provide liquidity when needed.

Embrace Flexible Savings Strategies:

To adapt to changing financial circumstances, embrace flexible savings strategies. This involves being open to adjusting your savings contributions based on varying income levels or expenses. During months with higher income, consider saving a larger percentage or amount. Conversely, if unexpected expenses arise, be prepared to temporarily reduce your savings contributions. The key is to maintain consistency in saving over the long term while allowing for short, term flexibility.

Diversify Your Investment Portfolio:

A flexible approach to investments involves diversifying your investment portfolio. Spread your investments across different asset classes, such as stocks, bonds, real estate, and mutual funds. Diversification helps mitigate risk and optimize returns. As your financial situation and goals evolve, rebalance your portfolio periodically to ensure alignment with your risk tolerance and objectives.

Stay Informed and Adapt to Market Conditions:

Financial markets are dynamic and can impact investment performance. Stay informed about market trends, economic indicators, and investment opportunities. Adapt your investment strategy based on market conditions and the performance of specific assets. Flexibility allows you to adjust your investment allocation, capitalize on emerging trends, or minimize exposure to declining sectors.

Consider Automatic Investment Plans:

Automatic investment plans are an effective tool for flexible savings and investments. These plans allow you to automate regular contributions to your investment accounts, such as retirement funds or brokerage accounts. Set up automatic transfers from your income or bank account, ensuring a consistent flow of funds into your investment portfolio. This approach simplifies the process and eliminates the temptation to deviate from your savings and investment goals.

Monitor and Review Regularly:

Flexibility in savings and investments requires regular monitoring and review. Keep track of your savings progress and investment performance. Assess whether you are on track to achieve your financial goals and if adjustments are necessary. Regular review empowers you to make informed decisions, capitalize on opportunities, and make necessary course corrections to stay aligned with your objectives.

Chapter Thirteen

Flexible Budgeting for Entrepreneurs

Unleashing Entrepreneurial Success: Harnessing Flexible Budgeting for Entrepreneurs

Entrepreneurs face unique challenges in managing their finances. With fluctuating income, uncertain expenses, and the need for strategic decision, making, entrepreneurs require a financial management approach that adapts to their dynamic business environment. Flexible budgeting is a powerful tool that allows entrepreneurs to effectively allocate resources, plan for growth, and navigate uncertainties. Below we will explore the benefits of flexible budgeting for entrepreneurs and discuss strategies to implement it successfully, empowering entrepreneurs to achieve financial success and drive their businesses forward.

Understand Your Business Model:

To effectively implement flexible budgeting, entrepreneurs must have a thorough understanding of their business model. Analyze revenue streams, cost structures, and cash flow patterns specific to your business. This understanding forms the foundation for developing a flexible budget that accurately reflects the financial dynamics of your business.

Plan for Variable Expenses:

Entrepreneurs often encounter variable expenses that can fluctuate based on business activities and market conditions. It is crucial to plan for these expenses within the flexible budget. Identify variable cost drivers, such as production materials, marketing campaigns, or inventory management, and allocate resources accordingly. By anticipating and planning for variable expenses, entrepreneurs can make informed decisions and adapt to changing business needs.

Incorporate Sensitivity Analysis:

Sensitivity analysis is a valuable technique for entrepreneurs to assess the impact of various scenarios on their financial performance. Introduce different assumptions into your budget, such as changes in sales volumes, pricing, or operating costs, and analyze the corresponding financial outcomes. This analysis helps entrepreneurs identify potential risks, evaluate opportunities, and make informed decisions that align with their business objectives.

Adopt a Rolling Budget Approach:

A rolling budget approach is particularly beneficial for entrepreneurs, given their dynamic business environment. Unlike traditional static budgets that cover a fixed period, a rolling budget continually updates and adjusts as new information becomes available. This approach allows entrepreneurs to incorporate real, time data, respond to market changes, and make timely adjustments to their financial plans.

Monitor Key Performance Indicators (KPIs):

Monitoring key performance indicators (KPIs) is crucial for entrepreneurs to track the financial health of their business. Identify and monitor KPIs that are relevant to your industry and business model. These could include metrics such as revenue growth, gross profit margin, customer acquisition cost, or cash conversion cycle. Regularly tracking KPIs provides valuable insights into your business's performance and helps you make data, driven decisions to drive growth and profitability.

Set Aside Funds for Business Development:

Entrepreneurs need to allocate funds for business development initiatives to fuel growth and innovation. Within the flexible budget, set aside a dedicated portion of your resources for activities such as research and development, product innovation, marketing campaigns, or expanding into new markets. By earmarking funds for business development, entrepreneurs can proactively invest in the future success of their ventures.

Manage Cash Flow Effectively:

Cash flow management is critical for entrepreneurial success. Entrepreneurs should project and monitor cash inflows and outflows meticulously. Consider implementing cash flow forecasting techniques to anticipate cash shortages or surpluses. This allows you to take proactive measures, such as securing additional funding or optimizing working capital, to ensure smooth operations and maintain financial stability.

Embrace Lean Financial Practices:

Lean financial practices, characterized by minimizing waste and maximizing efficiency, are highly beneficial for entrepreneurs. Look for opportunities to streamline processes, reduce unnecessary expenses, and optimize resource allocation. By adopting a lean mindset, entrepreneurs can maximize their financial resources and drive profitability.

Importance of Flexible Budgeting for Start

,

ups

Driving Start, up Success: The Crucial Role of Flexible Budgeting

Start, ups operate in a fast, paced and uncertain business landscape where financial management plays a pivotal role in their success. As new ventures navigate the challenges of limited resources, evolving market dynamics, and ambitious growth goals, adopting a flexible budgeting approach becomes essential. Flexible budgeting empowers start, ups to effectively allocate resources, make informed decisions, and adapt to changing circumstances. Below we will explore the importance of flexible budgeting for start, ups and discuss how it enables them to navigate the unique financial challenges they face.

Adjusting to Uncertain Revenues:

One of the key challenges for start, ups is uncertainty surrounding revenues. Flexible budgeting allows start, ups to anticipate and plan for varying revenue scenarios. By incorporating multiple revenue projections and sensitivity analysis into the budget, start, ups can better understand their revenue potential and allocate resources accordingly. This flexibility enables them to adapt quickly to changes in market demand and make strategic decisions to optimize revenue generation.

Optimizing Resource Allocation:

Start, ups typically have limited resources, making effective resource allocation critical for their survival and growth. Flexible budgeting enables start, ups to prioritize their spending based on their core business objectives. By analyzing the cost, benefit of different activities, start, ups can allocate resources to areas that drive the most value and support their growth strategy. This approach helps them maximize the impact of their resources and avoid wasteful spending.

Responding to Market Shifts:

Market conditions can change rapidly, especially in the early stages of a start, up. Flexible budgeting equips start, ups to respond to market shifts and adjust their strategies accordingly. By regularly reviewing their budgets and monitoring key performance indicators, start, ups can identify market trends, capitalize on emerging opportunities, and reallocate resources to meet changing customer demands. This agility enables start, ups to stay competitive and seize growth opportunities.

Managing Cash Flow Effectively:

Cash flow management is vital for start, ups, as cash shortages can quickly jeopardize their operations. Flexible budgeting provides start, ups with a comprehensive view of their cash flow, enabling them to project and plan their cash needs. By incorporating cash flow forecasting into their budgeting process, start, ups can anticipate potential cash gaps, take timely measures to bridge them, and maintain sufficient liquidity to support their day, to, day operations.

Controlling Costs and Burn Rate:

Start, ups often operate with limited funding, and controlling costs is crucial to extending their runway. Flexible budgeting helps start, ups closely monitor their expenses and manage their burn rate—the rate at which they consume their available funds. By tracking costs, identifying areas of inefficiency, and adjusting spending priorities, start, ups can optimize their cash utilization and extend their financial runway, providing them with more time to achieve sustainable growth.

Supporting Investor Relations:

Investors play a significant role in the growth journey of start, ups. Flexible budgeting enhances start, ups' ability to communicate their financial strategies effectively to investors. By developing and presenting a flexible budget, start, ups can demonstrate their financial acumen, strategic thinking, and their ability to adapt to changing circumstances. This builds confidence and trust with investors, increasing the likelihood of securing funding and attracting potential partnerships.

Evaluating Business Model Viability:

Start, ups often refine their business models through trial and error. Flexible budgeting helps start, ups evaluate the viability of their business models and make data, driven decisions. By comparing actual financial results against budgeted projections, start, ups can identify strengths, weaknesses, and areas for improvement in their business models. This iterative approach enables start, ups to fine, tune their strategies and increase their chances of achieving sustainable profitability.

Case Study: A Start

,

up's Success with Flexible Budgeting

Unveiling Success: A Start, up's Journey with Flexible Budgeting

Flexible budgeting plays a vital role in the success of start, ups by enabling effective financial management and strategic decision, making. Below we will explore a case study that highlights the success of a start, up that implemented flexible budgeting. The case study will demonstrate how the start, up utilized flexible budgeting to navigate financial challenges, optimize resource allocation, and achieve sustainable growth. Through this real, life example, we will uncover the power of flexible budgeting in driving the success of start, ups.

Case Study: XYZ Tech Solutions

XYZ Tech Solutions is a technology start, up that specializes in developing software solutions for small businesses. As a young company, XYZ Tech Solutions faced various financial challenges, including limited funding, uncertain revenue streams, and evolving market demands. To overcome these challenges, the company implemented a flexible budgeting approach that transformed its financial management and propelled its growth.

Adapting to Uncertain Revenues:

In its early stages, XYZ Tech Solutions faced uncertainty regarding customer demand and revenue projections. To address this, the company incorporated flexible budgeting techniques into its financial planning. By developing multiple revenue scenarios based on different market conditions and customer adoption rates, XYZ Tech Solutions gained a deeper understanding of its revenue potential. This allowed the company to allocate resources effectively, plan for contingencies, and adjust its strategies to align with the changing revenue landscape.

Optimizing Resource Allocation:

With limited resources, XYZ Tech Solutions recognized the importance of optimizing its resource allocation. Through flexible budgeting, the company carefully analyzed its cost structures, identified key cost drivers, and prioritized resource allocation based on the highest value, generating activities. By adopting a data, driven approach and continuously monitoring performance, XYZ Tech Solutions was able to allocate resources more efficiently, enhance operational efficiency, and maximize its return on investment.

Responding to Market Shifts:

The technology industry is characterized by rapid changes and evolving customer needs. XYZ Tech Solutions embraced flexible budgeting to respond to market shifts effectively. The company monitored market trends, customer feedback, and competitor activities, allowing it to adapt its product development and marketing strategies accordingly. By reallocating resources to capitalize on emerging opportunities and adjust its product roadmap, XYZ Tech Solutions maintained its competitive edge and stayed ahead of industry trends.

Managing Cash Flow Effectively:

Cash flow management is critical for the survival of start, ups. XYZ Tech Solutions leveraged flexible budgeting to effectively manage its cash flow. By closely monitoring its cash inflows and outflows, the company projected its cash needs and ensured sufficient liquidity to support its operations. Additionally, by integrating cash flow forecasting into its budgeting process, XYZ Tech Solutions proactively planned for potential cash gaps and implemented strategies to bridge them, ensuring the continuity of its operations.

Controlling Costs and Burn Rate:

XYZ Tech Solutions understood the importance of controlling costs and managing its burn rate. By incorporating flexible budgeting practices, the company closely tracked its expenses, identified areas of inefficiency, and adjusted its spending priorities. This proactive approach enabled XYZ Tech Solutions to optimize its cash utilization, extend its financial runway, and maintain financial stability during its growth phase. The company's focus on cost control played a pivotal role in its ability to achieve sustainable growth.

Supporting Investor Relations:

As XYZ Tech Solutions sought external funding, the implementation of flexible budgeting bolstered its investor relations. By presenting a comprehensive and flexible budget, the company demonstrated its financial acumen, strategic planning capabilities, and the ability to adapt to changing circumstances. The transparent and data, driven approach instilled confidence in potential investors, resulting in successful fundraising and strategic partnerships that further fueled the company's growth.

Tips for Entrepreneurs: Staying Flexible with Limited Resources

Thriving in Resource Constraints: Tips for Entrepreneurs to Stay Flexible

Entrepreneurs often face the challenge of operating with limited resources, whether it's funding, manpower, or time. In such resource, constrained environments, staying flexible becomes crucial for the success and growth of their ventures. Flexible budgeting plays a pivotal role in enabling entrepreneurs to optimize their resources, make agile decisions, and adapt to changing circumstances. Below we will discuss practical tips for entrepreneurs to stay flexible with limited resources, empowering them to navigate challenges effectively and drive their ventures forward.

Embrace Lean Principles:

Adopting lean principles is essential for entrepreneurs looking to stay flexible with limited resources. Lean methodology emphasizes minimizing waste, optimizing processes, and maximizing value. By eliminating non, essential activities, streamlining operations, and focusing on core value creation, entrepreneurs can conserve resources and improve efficiency. This approach allows them to allocate resources effectively and respond swiftly to market demands.

Prioritize Your Objectives:

When resources are limited, it's crucial to prioritize your objectives. Identify your key goals and focus your efforts on activities that directly contribute to their achievement. By aligning your resources with your top priorities, you can avoid spreading yourself too thin and ensure that your limited resources are allocated where they have the most significant impact.

Adopt a Flexible Budgeting Approach:

Flexible budgeting is a powerful tool for entrepreneurs with limited resources. Embrace a flexible budgeting approach that allows you to adjust your financial plans based on changing circumstances. Incorporate sensitivity analysis and multiple scenarios into your budget to anticipate potential challenges and make informed decisions. This approach empowers you to allocate resources dynamically, seize opportunities, and adapt your strategies to align with the evolving needs of your venture.

Leverage Technology:

Technology can be a game, changer for resource, constrained entrepreneurs. Embrace digital tools and software solutions that automate and streamline your operations. From project management platforms to customer relationship management (CRM) systems, technology can help you optimize processes, improve efficiency, and maximize the impact of your limited resources. Additionally, leverage online platforms for marketing, sales, and collaboration to expand your reach and reduce costs.

Build Strategic Partnerships:

Collaborating with strategic partners is an effective way to leverage external resources and expertise. Seek partnerships with complementary businesses or professionals who can provide support in areas where you have resource limitations. For example, partnering with a marketing agency can help you amplify your brand presence without investing heavily in an in, house marketing team. Strategic partnerships allow you to access additional resources, share costs, and accelerate growth.

Outsource Non, Core Activities:

Outsourcing non, core activities is a smart approach to optimize your resources. Identify tasks or functions that are not essential to your core competencies and consider outsourcing them to external service providers. This allows you to tap into specialized expertise without the need to hire full, time staff or invest in additional infrastructure. Outsourcing enables you to focus on strategic activities that directly contribute to the growth of your venture.

Continuously Evaluate and Adjust:

Resource constraints require entrepreneurs to be proactive in evaluating and adjusting their strategies. Continuously monitor and assess the performance of your business, identify areas of improvement, and adjust your plans accordingly. Regularly review your budget, analyze key performance indicators, and seek feedback from customers and stakeholders. This iterative approach enables you to make data, driven decisions, adapt to market dynamics, and optimize the utilization of your limited resources.

Foster a Culture of Innovation:

Innovation is a key driver of success for resource, constrained entrepreneurs. Encourage a culture of innovation within your team by promoting creative thinking, open communication, and experimentation. Empower your employees to generate innovative solutions that optimize resource utilization and overcome limitations.

Chapter Fourteen

Flexible Budgeting in the Public Sector

Driving Efficiency and Accountability: The Power of Flexible Budgeting in the Public Sector

Budgeting is a critical aspect of financial management in the public sector, enabling governments and public organizations to allocate resources and deliver essential services to citizens. Flexible budgeting has gained significant recognition as a tool for driving efficiency and accountability in the public sector. Below we will explore the concept of flexible budgeting in the public sector and discuss its benefits, challenges, and implementation strategies. By embracing flexible budgeting practices, governments and public organizations can enhance financial decision, making, optimize resource allocation, and achieve better outcomes for the communities they serve.

Adapting to Changing Priorities:

In the public sector, priorities and needs can evolve rapidly due to shifting demographics, emerging social issues, and changing government mandates. Flexible budgeting allows public organizations to adapt their financial plans to accommodate these changing priorities. By incorporating multiple scenarios and sensitivity analysis into the budgeting process, public sector entities can better understand the financial implications of different policy choices and adjust their resource allocation accordingly.

This flexibility enables them to respond to emerging needs and deliver services that align with the evolving demands of their communities.

Allocating Resources Based on Impact:

Flexible budgeting empowers public sector organizations to allocate resources based on the impact they aim to achieve. By setting clear goals and performance indicators, public entities can align their budgeting decisions with desired outcomes. This approach allows them to direct resources to programs and initiatives that have demonstrated effectiveness and deliver measurable results. By allocating resources based on impact, public organizations can ensure that taxpayer dollars are used efficiently and effectively to address the most pressing social and economic challenges.

Encouraging Innovation and Efficiency:

Flexible budgeting encourages innovation and efficiency in the public sector. By empowering public organizations to explore new approaches and funding models, flexible budgeting fosters a culture of innovation and continuous improvement. It enables public entities to explore alternative service delivery models, leverage technology, and adopt evidence, based practices to enhance efficiency and effectiveness. By encouraging innovation and efficiency, flexible budgeting helps public organizations deliver better services while optimizing the utilization of limited resources.

Enhancing Transparency and Accountability:

Transparency and accountability are fundamental principles in the public sector. Flexible budgeting promotes these principles by providing a clear line of sight between resource allocation decisions and outcomes. By involving stakeholders in the budgeting process and communicating budgetary decisions effectively, public organizations can enhance transparency and public trust. Furthermore, flexible budgeting enables better monitoring and evaluation of financial performance, allowing for increased accountability and the ability to make data, driven adjustments as needed.

Managing Uncertainty and Risk:

The public sector operates in an environment characterized by uncertainty and risk. Flexible budgeting equips public organizations with the tools to manage these challenges effectively. By incorporating risk assessments, scenario planning, and contingency funds into the budgeting process, public entities can proactively address potential risks and uncertainties. This approach enables them to develop strategies to mitigate risks, respond to unforeseen events, and maintain financial stability in the face of uncertainty.

Collaboration and Partnerships:

Flexible budgeting encourages collaboration and partnerships in the public sector. By engaging stakeholders, including citizens, community organizations, and private sector entities, public organizations can leverage additional resources and expertise. Collaboration allows for shared responsibilities, joint funding initiatives, and innovative problem, solving approaches. By embracing partnerships, public entities can extend the impact of their budgets and achieve collective outcomes that benefit the entire community.

Engaging Citizens and Communities:

Flexible budgeting provides opportunities for citizen engagement and participation in the budgeting process. By involving citizens in budget discussions, public organizations can ensure that budgetary decisions align with community priorities and values. This participatory approach fosters public trust, enhances accountability, and leads to better, informed budgeting decisions.

Challenges of Budgeting in Public Sector Organizations

Navigating the Budgeting Maze: Overcoming Challenges in Public Sector Budgeting

Budgeting is a complex process in the public sector, as governments and public organizations face unique challenges in managing public funds and delivering services to citizens. The process involves balancing competing priorities, addressing fiscal constraints, and ensuring accountability. Below we will explore the challenges of budgeting in public sector organizations and discuss how the adoption of flexible budgeting can help address these challenges. By understanding and overcoming these obstacles, public sector entities can achieve more effective and efficient resource allocation, leading to improved service delivery and citizen satisfaction.

Political Influence and Priorities:

One of the prominent challenges in public sector budgeting is the influence of political factors and competing priorities. The budgeting process can be subject to political pressures and short, term political objectives. This often leads to resource allocation decisions that may not align with long, term goals or citizen needs. Flexible budgeting can help address this challenge by incorporating multi, year planning and scenario analysis. By evaluating the financial impact of different policy choices and prioritizing based on evidence and citizen input, public sector organizations can overcome undue political influence and focus on delivering value to the community.

Complex Stakeholder Relationships:

Public sector organizations have a wide range of stakeholders with diverse interests and expectations. Budgeting decisions often involve engaging with multiple stakeholders, including elected officials, community groups, unions, and citizens. Balancing these competing interests and managing complex stakeholder relationships can pose challenges in the budgeting process. Flexible budgeting provides a framework for inclusive decision, making, allowing for stakeholder engagement and collaboration. By involving stakeholders early in the process and providing transparency in budget decisions, public sector organizations can foster trust, enhance accountability, and build consensus around resource allocation.

Fiscal Constraints and Revenue Volatility:

Public sector organizations often face fiscal constraints due to limited revenue sources and volatile economic conditions. This can result in funding gaps and challenges in maintaining service levels. Flexible budgeting can help address fiscal constraints by enabling organizations to forecast revenue fluctuations and adjust spending plans accordingly. By incorporating sensitivity analysis and contingency measures, public sector entities can mitigate the impact of revenue volatility and maintain essential services even in uncertain financial times.

Complex Program Evaluation:

Public sector organizations provide a wide range of programs and services, each with its own objectives, performance metrics, and evaluation criteria. Evaluating the effectiveness and efficiency of these programs is essential for informed budgeting decisions. However, program evaluation in the public sector can be complex and time, consuming, often requiring extensive data collection and analysis. Flexible budgeting facilitates program evaluation by incorporating performance measures, outcome, based budgeting, and data, driven decision, making. By linking budgeting decisions to program outcomes, public sector organizations can identify high, impact programs, reallocate resources, and improve overall program effectiveness.

Legacy Systems and Processes:

Many public sector organizations rely on legacy budgeting systems and processes that are outdated and inflexible. These systems may lack integration, limit data accessibility, and hinder collaboration among departments. Overcoming these challenges requires embracing modern technology and adopting flexible budgeting approaches that leverage data analytics, automation, and cloud, based systems. By implementing advanced budgeting software, public sector organizations can streamline their budgeting processes, enhance data transparency, and promote cross, departmental collaboration.

Performance Measurement and Accountability:

Public sector organizations are accountable to taxpayers and must demonstrate the efficient use of public funds. Establishing performance measures and monitoring outcomes can be challenging due to the complexity of public services and the difficulty in quantifying their impact. Flexible budgeting supports performance measurement by incorporating key performance indicators (KPIs) and outcome, based budgeting. By aligning resources with measurable performance goals, public sector organizations can improve accountability, identify areas for improvement, and make informed budgeting decisions that optimize service delivery.

The Role of Flexible Budgeting in Public Finance Management

Driving Effective Public Finance Management: The Power of Flexible Budgeting

Public finance management plays a crucial role in the efficient and accountable utilization of public funds. In the realm of public sector organizations, flexible budgeting has emerged as a valuable tool for enhancing financial planning, resource allocation, and overall performance. This chapter explores the role of flexible budgeting in public finance management and highlights its benefits, challenges, and implementation strategies. By embracing flexible budgeting, public sector entities can optimize their financial decision, making, adapt to changing circumstances, and achieve desired outcomes for the communities they serve.

Aligning Resources with Priorities:

Flexible budgeting enables public sector organizations to align their resources with priorities effectively. By incorporating multi, year planning, scenario analysis, and outcome, based budgeting, entities can ensure that available funds are allocated to areas that have the greatest impact. This approach allows for the strategic allocation of resources to programs and initiatives that align with the government's policy objectives and the needs of the citizens. By linking budgeting decisions to desired outcomes, public sector organizations can enhance their ability to achieve their goals efficiently.

Adapting to Changing Circumstances:

Public finance management is subject to dynamic environments with changing economic conditions, shifting societal needs, and evolving policy priorities. Flexible budgeting equips public sector organizations with the ability to adapt to these changes effectively. By incorporating flexibility into the budgeting process, entities can adjust their financial plans in response to emerging challenges or opportunities. This adaptability allows for the reallocation of resources, the introduction of new initiatives, and the modification of existing programs to better address the evolving needs of the public.

Improving Financial Forecasting:

Accurate financial forecasting is vital for effective public finance management. However, forecasting in the public sector can be challenging due to revenue volatility, uncertainty in expenditure patterns, and external economic factors. Flexible budgeting integrates forecasting techniques that consider different revenue scenarios, cost variations, and risk factors. By incorporating sensitivity analysis and contingency planning, public sector entities can improve their ability to forecast and anticipate potential financial fluctuations. This allows for better financial planning and the development of strategies to mitigate any adverse impacts.

Enhancing Accountability and Transparency:

Transparency and accountability are core principles of public finance management. Flexible budgeting enhances both by providing clear visibility into the allocation and utilization of public funds. It enables public sector organizations to communicate budgetary decisions to stakeholders, including citizens, elected officials, and oversight bodies. By involving stakeholders in the budgeting process, public entities can foster trust, increase awareness of resource allocation decisions, and ensure that public funds are used in a responsible and transparent manner.

Managing Fiscal Constraints:

Public sector organizations often operate within fiscal constraints, such as limited revenue sources and increasing demands for services. Flexible budgeting equips entities with the tools to manage these constraints effectively. By integrating fiscal sustainability analysis, expenditure reviews, and efficiency measures, public sector organizations can optimize their resource allocation and expenditure management. This helps mitigate the risks associated with fiscal constraints, promotes fiscal discipline, and enhances the long, term financial health of the organization.

Encouraging Performance, based Budgeting:

Performance, based budgeting is crucial for linking financial resources to desired outcomes and evaluating the effectiveness of public programs. Flexible budgeting facilitates performance, based budgeting by incorporating key performance indicators (KPIs), outcome measures, and monitoring mechanisms. This allows public sector organizations to assess the impact of their programs, make data, driven decisions, and allocate resources based on performance assessments. By emphasizing performance and results, entities can improve the efficiency and effectiveness of their public expenditures.

Case Study: Successful Implementation of a Flexible Budget in a Public Agency

Achieving Financial Agility: A Case Study of Successful Flexible Budget Implementation in a Public Agency

Flexible budgeting has gained recognition as a powerful tool for enhancing financial management in the public sector. It enables public agencies to adapt to changing circumstances, optimize resource allocation, and achieve desired outcomes. In this case study, we will explore the successful implementation of a flexible budget in a public agency, highlighting the challenges faced, strategies employed, and outcomes achieved. Through this case study, we aim to showcase the benefits and effectiveness of flexible budgeting in improving financial agility and performance in the public sector.

Case Study: City Department of Parks and Recreation

The City Department of Parks and Recreation (CDPR) is a public agency responsible for managing and maintaining the city's parks, recreational facilities, and public spaces. Faced with budget constraints and increasing demand for recreational services, the CDPR recognized the need for a more dynamic budgeting approach to optimize resource allocation and effectively address the evolving needs of the community.

Challenges Faced:

The CDPR faced several challenges that necessitated the implementation of a flexible budget. These challenges included limited funding, volatile revenue streams, and varying service demands throughout the year. Additionally, the agency encountered difficulties in aligning budgetary decisions with community priorities and achieving desired outcomes with traditional budgeting approaches.

Implementation Strategies:

Stakeholder Engagement: The CDPR initiated a comprehensive stakeholder engagement process to gather input from community members, park users, and local organizations. This engagement helped identify key priorities and ensure that budgetary decisions aligned with the needs and expectations of the community.

Performance Measures and Outcome, Based Budgeting: The CDPR developed a set of performance measures and outcome, based budgeting criteria to evaluate the effectiveness and efficiency of its programs and services. This approach allowed for better resource allocation decisions based on the anticipated impact and value delivered to the community.

Scenario Planning: The agency incorporated scenario planning into its budgeting process to account for potential changes in revenue, such as fluctuations in park usage fees and grants. By developing multiple scenarios, the CDPR could assess the financial implications of various situations and adjust resource allocation accordingly.

Continuous Monitoring and Evaluation: The CDPR established a robust monitoring and evaluation framework to track the performance of its programs and services against predefined goals and targets. Regular reviews allowed for data, driven decision, making and proactive adjustments to budgetary allocations based on actual performance.

Outcomes Achieved:

Improved Resource Allocation: The implementation of a flexible budget enabled the CDPR to optimize resource allocation based on community needs and program effectiveness. By aligning budgetary decisions with outcome, based criteria, the agency directed resources towards high, impact initiatives, resulting in improved service delivery and enhanced community satisfaction.

Financial Stability: The scenario planning component of the flexible budgeting process helped the CDPR anticipate and mitigate financial risks. By developing contingency plans and considering alternative revenue scenarios, the agency maintained financial stability even during periods of uncertainty, ensuring the continued provision of essential services.

Enhanced Accountability and Transparency: The CDPR's implementation of flexible budgeting increased accountability and transparency. Through stakeholder engagement and performance reporting, the agency communicated its budgetary decisions effectively, fostering trust among the community and demonstrating responsible use of public funds.

Adaptability to Changing Circumstances: The CDPR's flexible budgeting approach allowed for quick adjustments in response to changing circumstances. For example, during the COVID, 19 pandemic, the agency swiftly reallocated resources to support virtual recreational programs and ensure the safety of park visitors. This adaptability enabled the CDPR to continue serving the community effectively despite unforeseen challenges.

Data, Informed Decision, making: The implementation of performance measures and outcome, based budgeting provided the CDPR with valuable data to inform decision, making.

Chapter Fifteen

Beyond Budgeting: A Radical Alternative?

Traditional budgeting has long been the standard approach for financial planning and resource allocation in organizations. However, in recent years, the concept of "beyond budgeting" has emerged as a radical alternative that challenges the traditional budgeting paradigm. This chapter explores the concept of beyond budgeting and its relationship with flexible budgeting. We will examine the principles, benefits, challenges, and potential implications of adopting a beyond budgeting approach. By delving into this alternative perspective, organizations can explore new avenues for achieving agility, adaptability, and improved performance.

The Traditional Budgeting Paradigm:

Traditional budgeting is a fixed and often annual process that involves setting targets, allocating resources, and monitoring financial performance. It operates on the assumption that future conditions and business environments can be accurately predicted and that budgets should be strictly adhered to throughout the period. However, critics argue that traditional budgeting is inherently flawed, as it can lead to rigid decision, making, lack of agility, and a focus on meeting arbitrary targets rather than responding to actual needs and market dynamics.

The Beyond Budgeting Approach:

Beyond budgeting represents a departure from the traditional budgeting paradigm. It emphasizes a more dynamic and adaptive approach to financial management. The core principles of beyond budgeting include:

Flexible Targets: Beyond budgeting challenges the notion of fixed targets by advocating for dynamic and rolling forecasts. It recognizes that the future is uncertain and that targets should be continuously adjusted based on changing circumstances and market conditions.

Decentralized Decision, making: Beyond budgeting encourages decentralized decision, making by empowering frontline managers and teams to make decisions that align with the organization's strategic objectives. This approach allows for more rapid and context, specific decision, making, fostering agility and responsiveness.

Relative Benchmarking: Rather than comparing performance against fixed targets, beyond budgeting promotes relative benchmarking. This involves comparing performance against peers, best practices, or market conditions. It encourages organizations to focus on continuous improvement and learning rather than meeting predefined goals.

Dynamic Resource Allocation: Beyond budgeting emphasizes dynamic resource allocation based on strategic priorities and value creation. It advocates for resource allocation decisions to be made in real, time, considering market opportunities and changing customer needs.

Benefits of Beyond Budgeting:

Enhanced Agility: Beyond budgeting enables organizations to respond more quickly to changing market conditions, emerging opportunities, and potential threats. By adopting a flexible and dynamic approach, organizations can make timely decisions and adjust resource allocation to capture new opportunities or mitigate risks.

Improved Decision, making: Decentralized decision, making in beyond budgeting allows for faster and more informed decision, making. Frontline managers have a better understanding of their operational realities and can make decisions based on real, time information. This fosters innovation, accountability, and a sense of ownership among employees.

Focus on Value Creation: Beyond budgeting shifts the focus from meeting arbitrary targets to value creation. By adopting relative benchmarking, organizations can strive for continuous improvement and compare themselves to the best performers in their industry. This encourages a mindset of innovation and a relentless pursuit of excellence.

Better Resource Allocation: The dynamic resource allocation approach of beyond budgeting ensures that resources are directed to activities that generate the most value. By reallocating resources based on changing priorities and market conditions, organizations can optimize their investment decisions and achieve better financial performance.

Challenges and Implications:

Despite the benefits, adopting a beyond budgeting approach is not without challenges. Some of the potential challenges include:

Cultural Shift: Shifting from traditional budgeting to beyond budgeting requires a significant cultural transformation within the organization. It requires a shift from a command, and, control management style to one that promotes empowerment, trust, and collaboration.

Understanding the Beyond Budgeting Model

Understanding the Beyond Budgeting Model: Embracing Agility and Adaptive Management

The traditional budgeting model has long been the go, to framework for financial planning and control in organizations. However, the concept of beyond budgeting has emerged as an alternative approach that challenges the limitations of traditional budgeting. Beyond budgeting advocates for a more flexible, agile, and adaptive management model that promotes responsiveness to dynamic business environments. This chapter explores the principles, benefits, and implications of the beyond budgeting model and its relation to flexible budgeting. By understanding this innovative approach, organizations can unlock their potential for continuous improvement, innovation, and enhanced performance.

The Principles of Beyond Budgeting:

The beyond budgeting model is built on a set of guiding principles that fundamentally challenge the traditional budgeting paradigm. These principles include:

Adaptive Management: Beyond budgeting recognizes the dynamic nature of business environments and the inherent uncertainty they bring. It emphasizes the need for organizations to embrace adaptive management practices that allow for continuous learning, experimentation, and adjustment. This principle promotes agility in decision, making and resource allocation.

Decentralized Authority: Beyond budgeting encourages the decentralization of decision, making authority to empower frontline managers and teams. By providing autonomy and responsibility to those closest to the action, organizations can respond more effectively to customer needs, market trends, and emerging opportunities.

Relative Targets and Benchmarking: Beyond budgeting suggests shifting from fixed targets to relative targets and benchmarking. Rather than rigidly adhering to predefined goals, organizations should focus on relative performance against peers, industry best practices, and changing market conditions. This principle promotes a culture of continuous improvement and fosters innovation and learning.

Rolling Forecasts: Beyond budgeting challenges the annual budgeting cycle by advocating for rolling forecasts. Instead of rigid, fixed budgets, organizations regularly update their forecasts based on the latest information, allowing for more accurate and dynamic resource allocation decisions.

Benefits of the Beyond Budgeting Model:

Improved Responsiveness: By embracing adaptive management practices, organizations can respond more quickly and effectively to changes in the business environment. Beyond budgeting enables organizations to adjust their strategies, resource allocations, and priorities in real, time, ensuring they remain relevant and competitive.

Enhanced Decision, making: Decentralized decision, making empowers employees at all levels of the organization to make informed decisions based on their unique perspectives and knowledge. This fosters a culture of ownership, accountability, and innovation, leading to more effective and timely decision, making.

Greater Flexibility: The beyond budgeting model offers organizations the flexibility to allocate resources based on changing priorities and evolving market conditions. With rolling forecasts, organizations can reallocate resources to seize new opportunities, address emerging challenges, and ensure the efficient utilization of resources.

Continuous Improvement: By adopting relative targets and benchmarking, organizations shift their focus from meeting predetermined goals to continuous improvement. This encourages a mindset of learning, innovation, and finding new ways to deliver value to customers and stakeholders.

Implications of the Beyond Budgeting Model:

Implementing the beyond budgeting model is not without its challenges and implications. Organizations must be prepared for the following:

Cultural Transformation: Moving away from traditional budgeting requires a cultural shift within the organization. It involves embracing transparency, trust, and a willingness to experiment and learn from both successes and failures. This cultural transformation may require extensive communication, training, and support to ensure buy, in and alignment across the organization.

Performance Measurement: Beyond budgeting requires a shift in performance measurement practices. Rather than solely relying on financial metrics, organizations must develop a balanced set of key performance indicators (KPIs) that align with strategic objectives and desired outcomes. This ensures that performance measurement reflects the organization's overall success in delivering value.

Comparing Flexible Budgeting with Beyond Budgeting

Comparing Flexible Budgeting with Beyond Budgeting: Finding the Right Fit for Organizational Agility

In the realm of modern financial management, both flexible budgeting and beyond budgeting have emerged as alternative approaches to traditional budgeting. While they share a common goal of enhancing organizational agility and adaptability, they differ in their underlying principles and methodologies. This chapter aims to compare and contrast flexible budgeting with beyond budgeting, shedding light on their respective features, benefits, and considerations. By understanding the unique characteristics of each approach, organizations can make informed decisions about which framework aligns best with their goals and objectives.

Flexible Budgeting: A Dynamic Resource Allocation Tool

Flexible budgeting is a widely practiced approach that allows organizations to adjust their budgets based on actual activity levels or changing circumstances. It involves the creation of flexible budgets that can be modified throughout the budgeting period to reflect the actual levels of activity. The key features of flexible budgeting include:

Activity, Based Planning: Flexible budgeting aligns budgeting decisions with varying levels of activity. It takes into account different factors that influence costs and revenues, enabling organizations to forecast and plan accordingly.

Resource Optimization: By adjusting the budget to reflect the actual levels of activity, organizations can optimize resource allocation. This ensures that resources are allocated effectively to areas that require additional support and avoids over or underutilization of resources.

Performance Evaluation: Flexible budgeting facilitates performance evaluation by comparing actual results with the flexible budget. It provides insights into the efficiency and effectiveness of resource utilization, enabling organizations to make informed decisions for improvement.

Benefits of Flexible Budgeting:

Adaptability: Flexible budgeting allows organizations to adapt quickly to changing circumstances. It provides a framework for adjusting resources and priorities in response to fluctuations in activity levels or external factors, ensuring that budgets remain relevant and aligned with organizational goals.

Accurate Forecasting: By considering varying levels of activity, flexible budgeting enhances the accuracy of forecasting. It provides a more realistic representation of future costs and revenues, enabling organizations to make better, informed decisions.

Cost Control: Flexible budgeting facilitates better cost control by identifying areas of inefficiency or cost overruns. It enables organizations to analyze and address deviations from the budgeted amounts, leading to improved financial performance.

Beyond Budgeting: A Paradigm Shift in Management

Beyond budgeting represents a radical departure from traditional budgeting practices. It advocates for a more adaptive and decentralized management model, emphasizing principles such as dynamic resource allocation and relative performance measurement. The key features of beyond budgeting include:

Dynamic Planning and Forecasting: Beyond budgeting promotes continuous planning and forecasting, moving away from the fixed and annual budgeting cycle. Rolling forecasts are used to update targets and resource allocations in response to changing circumstances.

Decentralized Decision, making: Beyond budgeting encourages decentralized decision, making, empowering frontline managers and teams to make decisions based on their knowledge and expertise. This approach fosters accountability, innovation, and responsiveness.

Relative Performance Measurement: Instead of relying solely on fixed targets, beyond budgeting emphasizes relative performance measurement. Organizations benchmark their performance against industry peers, best practices, and changing market conditions, fostering a continuous improvement mindset.

Benefits of Beyond Budgeting:

Agility and Adaptability: Beyond budgeting enables organizations to adapt quickly to changing environments. By utilizing rolling forecasts and empowering decision, makers at all levels, organizations can respond to market dynamics and seize emerging opportunities more effectively.

Innovation and Empowerment: Decentralized decision, making fosters a culture of innovation and empowers employees to contribute to the organization's success. This approach encourages creative problem, solving, collaboration, and a sense of ownership among employees.

Evaluating the Applicability of Beyond Budgeting

Evaluating the Applicability of Beyond Budgeting: A Pragmatic Perspective

Beyond budgeting has gained attention as a radical alternative to traditional budgeting practices, emphasizing flexibility, decentralized decision, making, and adaptive management. While the principles and benefits of beyond budgeting are compelling, it is essential to evaluate its applicability in different organizational contexts. This chapter aims to critically examine the suitability and challenges of implementing beyond budgeting, considering its relation to flexible budgeting. By assessing its applicability, organizations can make informed decisions about whether and how to adopt the beyond budgeting approach.

Understanding Beyond Budgeting:

Beyond budgeting is based on the premise that traditional budgeting is rigid, bureaucratic, and often disconnected from the dynamic realities of business environments. It advocates for a more adaptive, responsive, and decentralized management model. Key principles of beyond budgeting include:

Adaptive Planning: Beyond budgeting suggests the use of rolling forecasts and continuous planning to adapt to changing circumstances. Instead of fixed annual budgets, organizations update their forecasts regularly to align resources with current conditions.

Decentralized Decision, making: Beyond budgeting promotes empowerment and autonomy by delegating decision, making authority to frontline managers and teams. This enables faster responses to market conditions, encourages innovation, and enhances employee engagement.

Relative Performance Measurement: Beyond budgeting challenges the fixation on meeting predetermined targets and emphasizes relative performance measurement. Rather than comparing against fixed budgets, organizations benchmark their performance against industry peers and best practices, fostering a continuous improvement mindset.

Applicability of Beyond Budgeting:

Organizational Culture: Implementing beyond budgeting requires a supportive organizational culture that values transparency, trust, and collaboration. It may be more easily embraced in organizations with an existing culture of empowerment and open communication.

Industry Dynamics: The applicability of beyond budgeting varies across industries. Organizations operating in rapidly changing, innovative sectors may find it more suitable due to their need for agility and adaptability. However, industries with stable environments or stringent regulatory requirements may face challenges in implementing beyond budgeting.

Size and Complexity: The size and complexity of an organization can impact the applicability of beyond budgeting. Large organizations with multiple business units or global operations may face challenges in coordinating decentralized decision, making and aligning strategic objectives.

Leadership Commitment: Successful implementation of beyond budgeting requires strong leadership commitment and clear communication. Leaders must be willing to challenge traditional practices, support cultural transformation, and provide the necessary resources and training.

Challenges of Implementing Beyond Budgeting:

Cultural Shift: Shifting from traditional budgeting to beyond budgeting requires a significant cultural transformation. Resistance to change, fear of losing control, and a preference for stability may pose challenges in overcoming organizational inertia.

Performance Measurement: Beyond budgeting challenges traditional performance measurement practices that rely heavily on financial targets. Developing new performance metrics that align with strategic objectives and encourage continuous improvement can be complex and time, consuming.

Information Systems: Implementing beyond budgeting often requires organizations to enhance their information systems and data analytics capabilities. Real, time data availability, forecasting tools, and performance dashboards are essential to support decentralized decision, making and resource allocation.

External Factors: External factors, such as legal and regulatory requirements, may pose challenges to the implementation of beyond budgeting. Organizations operating in highly regulated industries or facing compliance constraints may find it difficult to fully adopt the decentralized decision, making aspect of beyond budgeting.

Integration with Flexible Budgeting:

While beyond budgeting and flexible budgeting share the goal of enhancing organizational agility, they differ in their approach. Flexible budgeting focuses on adjusting budgets based on actual activity levels, while beyond budgeting promotes dynamic planning, decentralized decision, making, and relative performance measurement.

Chapter Sixteen

Implementing a Flexible Budgeting System

Implementing a Flexible Budgeting System: Navigating the Path to Financial Agility

In today's fast, paced and ever, changing business landscape, organizations are increasingly recognizing the need for flexible budgeting systems. A flexible budgeting system allows organizations to adjust their budgets based on actual activity levels and changing market conditions. Implementing such a system requires careful planning, stakeholder involvement, and robust financial management processes. This chapter explores the key considerations and steps involved in implementing a flexible budgeting system, highlighting its importance in enhancing financial agility and performance.

Assessing Organizational Readiness:

Before embarking on the implementation of a flexible budgeting system, organizations need to assess their readiness for change. This involves evaluating the current budgeting process, understanding the organization's culture and appetite for flexibility, and identifying key stakeholders who will play a role in the implementation process. It is essential to secure leadership buy, in and establish a clear vision for the benefits of adopting a flexible budgeting system.

Defining Objectives and Metrics:

Clearly defining objectives and metrics is crucial in aligning the flexible budgeting system with organizational goals. This involves identifying key performance indicators (KPIs) that reflect the organization's strategic priorities and desired outcomes. Objectives and metrics should be specific, measurable, achievable, relevant, and time, bound (SMART), enabling effective monitoring and evaluation of performance.

Designing the Flexible Budgeting Framework:

The next step is to design the flexible budgeting framework. This involves determining the appropriate time period for budgeting (e.g., monthly, quarterly), establishing the baseline budget, and developing guidelines for adjusting the budget based on changing activity levels. The framework should be adaptable, allowing for modifications as per organizational needs and external market conditions.

Gathering and Analyzing Data:

Implementing a flexible budgeting system requires robust data gathering and analysis processes. Organizations need to collect and analyze historical data related to revenues, costs, and activity levels to develop accurate baseline budgets. Additionally, organizations should consider external factors, such as market trends and industry benchmarks, to inform the budgeting process.

Establishing a Continuous Forecasting Process:

A key element of a flexible budgeting system is the establishment of a continuous forecasting process. This involves regularly updating forecasts based on actual performance and changing circumstances. By incorporating rolling forecasts, organizations can adjust their budgets to reflect real, time information, ensuring the accuracy and relevance of budgetary decisions.

Training and Education:

To ensure successful implementation, organizations must invest in training and education. Employees at all levels should be equipped with the necessary knowledge and skills to understand and utilize the flexible budgeting system effectively. Training sessions, workshops, and documentation can help foster a shared understanding and create a culture of financial responsibility and accountability.

Implementing Robust Financial Controls:

Implementing a flexible budgeting system requires the establishment of robust financial controls. This includes defining approval processes, monitoring budget variances, and conducting regular performance reviews. By implementing effective financial controls, organizations can identify deviations from the budget and take corrective actions in a timely manner.

Continuous Evaluation and Improvement:

The implementation of a flexible budgeting system is an ongoing process that requires continuous evaluation and improvement. Organizations should regularly assess the effectiveness of the system, solicit feedback from stakeholders, and make necessary adjustments. This iterative approach ensures that the flexible budgeting system remains aligned with the evolving needs of the organization.

Benefits of Implementing a Flexible Budgeting System:

Enhanced Decision, making: A flexible budgeting system provides organizations with timely and accurate information, enabling informed decision, making. Adjusting budgets based on actual activity levels allows organizations to allocate resources effectively, identify cost, saving opportunities, and seize emerging opportunities.

Improved Financial Performance: By aligning budgets with actual activity levels and market conditions, organizations can improve financial performance.

The Role of Leadership in Budgeting Process Change

The Role of Leadership in Budgeting Process Change: Driving Success in Flexible Budgeting

Budgeting process change, particularly in the context of implementing flexible budgeting, requires strong leadership and a commitment to driving organizational transformation. The role of leadership is crucial in shaping the budgeting process, fostering a culture of flexibility, and driving the successful implementation of flexible budgeting practices. This chapter explores the key aspects of leadership in budgeting process change, highlighting the importance of leadership behaviors, communication, and organizational alignment in achieving success.

Setting the Vision and Direction:

Effective leaders play a pivotal role in setting the vision and direction for budgeting process change. They articulate the reasons for adopting flexible budgeting, highlight its benefits, and create a compelling case for change. By clearly communicating the strategic objectives and the need for increased flexibility, leaders inspire confidence and build a shared understanding among stakeholders.

Creating a Culture of Flexibility:

Leadership is instrumental in fostering a culture of flexibility within the organization. This involves encouraging innovation, risk, taking, and adaptability. Leaders set the tone by embracing change themselves, encouraging open dialogue, and creating an environment where employees feel empowered to challenge traditional budgeting practices and propose new ideas.

Stakeholder Engagement and Collaboration:

Leadership plays a critical role in engaging and collaborating with key stakeholders throughout the budgeting process change. They involve stakeholders at all levels, including finance teams, department heads, and operational staff, to gather insights, address concerns, and gain buy, in. By involving stakeholders early on and seeking their input, leaders build trust and foster a sense of ownership among the workforce.

Communication and Transparency:

Effective communication is paramount in budgeting process change. Leaders must consistently communicate the rationale, progress, and benefits of flexible budgeting to all stakeholders. Transparent communication fosters understanding, reduces resistance to change, and aligns the organization towards the common goal of implementing flexible budgeting practices.

Providing Resources and Support:

Leadership plays a vital role in providing the necessary resources, both financial and human, to support the implementation of flexible budgeting. This includes investing in training programs, data analytics tools, and technology infrastructure to enable accurate forecasting, real, time reporting, and data, driven decision, making. Leaders also allocate sufficient time and manpower to ensure successful implementation.

Leading by Example:

Leadership by example is a powerful driver of change. When leaders demonstrate a commitment to flexible budgeting practices, such as adjusting budgets based on changing circumstances, allocating resources effectively, and embracing continuous improvement, they set the tone for the entire organization. Leading by example encourages others to embrace the change and reinforces the importance of flexibility in budgeting.

Performance Evaluation and Accountability:

Leadership is responsible for establishing performance evaluation mechanisms and holding individuals and teams accountable for achieving budgeting goals. By setting clear expectations, monitoring progress, and providing regular feedback, leaders ensure that the flexible budgeting process is on track and aligned with organizational objectives.

Continuous Learning and Improvement:

Leadership should promote a culture of continuous learning and improvement in the budgeting process. They encourage teams to evaluate the effectiveness of flexible budgeting practices, identify areas for improvement, and share best practices. By fostering a learning, oriented mindset, leaders enable the organization to adapt and refine its budgeting processes over time.

The Impact of Leadership in Budgeting Process Change:

Effective leadership in budgeting process change can yield several positive outcomes for the organization:

Improved Decision, making: Leadership plays a crucial role in providing the vision, guidance, and information necessary for informed decision, making. Flexible budgeting allows leaders to make data, driven decisions based on real, time information, enabling them to respond quickly to market fluctuations and changing business conditions.

Training and Development for Effective Flexible Budgeting

Training and Development for Effective Flexible Budgeting: Empowering Financial Agility

Implementing flexible budgeting practices requires a knowledgeable and skilled workforce capable of navigating dynamic financial landscapes. Training and development play a crucial role in equipping employees with the necessary competencies to effectively engage in flexible budgeting processes. This chapter explores the importance of training and development in the context of flexible budgeting, highlighting key areas of focus and strategies for building expertise in financial agility.

Understanding the Principles of Flexible Budgeting:

To effectively engage in flexible budgeting, employees need a solid understanding of its principles and concepts. Training programs should introduce the fundamental concepts of flexible budgeting, such as adjusting budgets based on activity levels, using rolling forecasts, and aligning budgets with strategic objectives. This foundational knowledge enables employees to grasp the underlying principles and rationale of flexible budgeting.

Financial Analysis and Forecasting Skills:

Financial analysis and forecasting are essential competencies for effective flexible budgeting. Training programs should focus on developing employees' skills in analyzing financial data, identifying trends, and forecasting future outcomes. This includes training in data interpretation, financial modeling techniques, and the use of forecasting tools and software. By enhancing employees' financial analysis and forecasting capabilities, organizations can make informed budgetary decisions in a dynamic business environment.

Communication and Collaboration:

Effective communication and collaboration are critical for successful flexible budgeting. Training programs should emphasize interpersonal and communication skills to foster collaboration among teams, departments, and stakeholders. This includes training in active listening, effective communication techniques, and cross, functional collaboration. Building strong communication and collaboration skills facilitates the exchange of information, aligns diverse perspectives, and ensures a shared understanding of budgetary goals and strategies.

Change Management and Adaptability:

Training and development programs should address change management and adaptability skills, as implementing flexible budgeting involves significant process and mindset shifts. Employees need to understand the benefits of flexible budgeting, navigate resistance to change, and embrace a culture of adaptability. Training in change management methodologies, resilience, and problem, solving equips employees with the skills to navigate the challenges associated with implementing flexible budgeting practices.

Data Analytics and Technology Proficiency:

In the era of digital transformation, data analytics and technology proficiency are crucial for effective flexible budgeting. Training programs should provide employees with the necessary knowledge and skills to leverage data analytics tools, financial software, and reporting platforms. This includes training in data interpretation, data visualization techniques, and advanced Excel skills. Proficiency in data analytics and technology empowers employees to analyze financial data, generate insights, and make data, driven decisions.

Continuous Learning and Professional Development:

Flexible budgeting requires a mindset of continuous learning and professional development. Organizations should encourage employees to engage in ongoing learning opportunities, such as workshops, webinars, and industry conferences focused on budgeting best practices and financial management. Providing access to relevant resources and encouraging employees to pursue professional certifications and qualifications fosters a culture of continuous improvement and ensures that employees stay up, to, date with evolving industry trends.

Role, playing and Simulations:

Role, playing and simulations offer employees hands, on experience in applying flexible budgeting techniques in a controlled environment. These interactive training methods allow participants to practice decision, making, analyze financial scenarios, and adjust budgets based on changing conditions. Role, playing exercises facilitate skill development in real, time, encouraging employees to apply their knowledge and build confidence in making flexible budgeting decisions.

Performance Evaluation and Feedback:

Training and development programs should incorporate performance evaluation and feedback mechanisms to assess employees' understanding and application of flexible budgeting concepts. This may involve quizzes, case studies, or practical exercises where employees demonstrate their proficiency in flexible budgeting. Providing constructive feedback helps employees identify areas for improvement and reinforces the importance of continuous learning and development.

Measuring the Success of Your Flexible Budget Implementation

Measuring the Success of Your Flexible Budget Implementation: Evaluating Financial Agility

Implementing a flexible budgeting system is a transformative process that can greatly enhance an organization's financial agility. However, it is essential to measure the success of this implementation to ensure that the desired outcomes are achieved. Measuring the success of flexible budget implementation involves assessing key performance indicators, evaluating financial performance, and gathering feedback from stakeholders. This chapter explores the importance of measuring the success of flexible budget implementation and highlights key metrics and evaluation methods.

Key Performance Indicators (KPIs):

Establishing relevant key performance indicators is vital in measuring the success of flexible budget implementation. KPIs should align with the organization's strategic objectives and reflect the desired outcomes of implementing flexible budgeting practices. Examples of KPIs include variance analysis, revenue growth, cost containment, return on investment, and cash flow stability. These indicators provide a quantitative assessment of the effectiveness of the flexible budgeting system and its impact on financial performance.

Financial Performance Evaluation:

Evaluating financial performance is a critical component of measuring the success of flexible budget implementation. This involves comparing actual financial results against the flexible budget and analyzing variances. Variances indicate deviations from the budgeted amounts and can provide valuable insights into areas of strength or areas that require improvement. By conducting regular financial performance evaluations, organizations can identify trends, assess the accuracy of forecasting, and make informed decisions to optimize resource allocation.

Stakeholder Feedback and Engagement:

Gathering feedback from stakeholders is an essential qualitative measure of the success of flexible budget implementation. Engaging stakeholders, such as department heads, finance teams, and operational staff, allows organizations to understand their perspectives on the effectiveness and impact of the flexible budgeting system. Surveys, interviews, and focus groups can be utilized to gather feedback, identify challenges, and uncover opportunities for improvement. Stakeholder feedback provides valuable insights into the practical application of the flexible budgeting system and helps identify areas for refinement.

Continuous Improvement Initiatives:

Measuring the success of flexible budget implementation should involve a focus on continuous improvement. Organizations should establish a culture of ongoing evaluation and learning, encouraging employees to identify areas where the flexible budgeting system can be enhanced. This may involve soliciting suggestions for improvement, conducting post, implementation reviews, and implementing process refinements based on feedback received. Continuous improvement initiatives ensure that the flexible budgeting system evolves alongside the changing needs of the organization.

Compliance with Financial Regulations and Standards:

Another aspect of measuring the success of flexible budget implementation is ensuring compliance with financial regulations and standards.

Organizations should evaluate whether the implementation aligns with industry, specific regulations and financial reporting requirements. This involves assessing the accuracy and reliability of financial information, adherence to accounting principles, and compliance with applicable laws. Compliance assessments provide assurance that the flexible budgeting system is operating within the boundaries of legal and regulatory frameworks.

Employee Satisfaction and Engagement:

The satisfaction and engagement of employees play a vital role in the success of flexible budget implementation. Organizations can measure employee satisfaction through surveys, focus groups, or performance evaluations. High levels of employee satisfaction and engagement indicate that the flexible budgeting system is positively received and effectively understood by the workforce. Additionally, organizations can assess employee engagement by monitoring the implementation of budgeting practices, employee involvement in decision, making processes, and the adoption of innovative ideas suggested by employees.

Benchmarking and External Comparison:

Benchmarking and external comparison allow organizations to assess the success of flexible budget implementation in relation to industry standards and peers. This involves gathering information on best practices, conducting benchmarking studies, and participating in industry surveys. By comparing performance metrics, cost efficiencies, and financial outcomes with other organizations, organizations can identify areas of improvement and gain insights into leading practices in flexible budget implementation.

Chapter Seventeen

The Ethics of Flexible Budgeting

The Ethics of Flexible Budgeting: Balancing Financial Flexibility and Accountability

Flexible budgeting is a dynamic approach that allows organizations to adapt their budgets to changing circumstances. While the focus is often on the financial benefits and strategic advantages of flexible budgeting, it is equally important to consider the ethical implications. Ethical considerations in flexible budgeting revolve around transparency, fairness, accountability, and the responsible use of resources. This chapter explores the ethics of flexible budgeting and highlights the key principles that organizations should uphold to ensure ethical practices.

Transparency and Disclosure:

Transparency is a fundamental ethical principle in flexible budgeting. Organizations must provide clear and accurate information about the budgeting process, assumptions, and adjustments made in response to changing conditions. Transparent communication ensures that stakeholders understand the rationale behind budget decisions and can hold the organization accountable. Disclosure of budget revisions, variances, and the impact on financial outcomes promotes trust and fosters ethical behavior.

Fairness and Equity:

Flexible budgeting should prioritize fairness and equity in resource allocation. Ethical considerations require organizations to distribute resources in a manner that is fair, just, and aligned with organizational goals. This means avoiding bias or favoritism in budget adjustments and ensuring that all departments or projects have equal opportunities to access resources. Fairness in budgeting promotes a sense of trust and fosters a positive organizational culture.

Accountability and Responsibility:

Accountability and responsibility are ethical imperatives in flexible budgeting. Leaders and decision, makers should be accountable for the budget decisions they make and take responsibility for the outcomes. This includes monitoring the actual performance against budgeted targets, identifying and addressing variances, and providing explanations for deviations. Accountability ensures that budgeting decisions are made with integrity and align with the organization's values.

Ethical Considerations in Budget Adjustments:

Budget adjustments are a key aspect of flexible budgeting. However, ethical considerations should guide the process of making these adjustments. Organizations should carefully evaluate the impact of budget revisions on various stakeholders, such as employees, customers, and the wider community. Considerations should include the potential consequences for employees' job security, the quality of products or services, and the organization's reputation. Ethical budget adjustments prioritize the well, being of stakeholders and avoid detrimental impacts.

Responsible Use of Resources:

Ethical flexible budgeting emphasizes responsible use of resources. Organizations should consider the social and environmental impact of budgeting decisions. This includes avoiding unnecessary waste, promoting sustainability, and making responsible choices that align with corporate social responsibility (CSR) principles. Responsible resource allocation ensures that organizations contribute positively to society and the environment while achieving their financial objectives.

Ethical Decision, Making Processes:

Ethical flexible budgeting requires organizations to establish robust decision, making processes. These processes should incorporate ethical guidelines, promote open dialogue, and encourage diverse perspectives. Ethical decision, making frameworks, such as stakeholder analysis or cost, benefit analysis, can help organizations evaluate the ethical implications of budgeting decisions. By involving key stakeholders in the decision, making process and considering their interests, organizations can make informed and ethical choices.

Ethical Leadership:

Leadership plays a crucial role in promoting ethical flexible budgeting practices. Ethical leaders uphold the organization's values, lead by example, and create a culture of integrity and ethical decision, making. Leaders should emphasize the importance of ethics in budgeting processes, provide training and guidance on ethical practices, and ensure that ethical considerations are integrated into the overall budgeting framework.

External Auditing and Oversight:

External auditing and oversight mechanisms contribute to the ethical dimension of flexible budgeting. Independent audits of budgeting processes and financial statements provide assurance that ethical standards are being upheld. External oversight, such as regulatory bodies or governance committees, can help monitor and enforce ethical practices in budgeting.

Understanding Ethical Considerations in Budgeting

Understanding Ethical Considerations in Budgeting: Upholding Integrity and Responsibility

Budgeting is a critical process that involves allocating financial resources to achieve organizational goals. While the focus is often on financial outcomes, it is essential to recognize the ethical considerations that underpin budgeting decisions. Ethical considerations in budgeting revolve around fairness, transparency, accountability, and responsible resource allocation. This chapter explores the ethical aspects of budgeting, with a particular emphasis on flexible budgeting, and highlights key principles that organizations should consider to ensure ethical practices.

Fairness and Equity:

Fairness and equity are fundamental ethical principles in budgeting. Organizations should strive to distribute resources in a manner that is fair, just, and aligned with organizational goals. This means avoiding biases or favoritism in resource allocation and ensuring equal opportunities for departments or projects to access resources. Fairness in budgeting promotes a sense of trust, enhances employee morale, and fosters a positive organizational culture.

Transparency and Accountability:

Transparency and accountability are crucial ethical considerations in budgeting. Organizations should maintain transparency by providing clear and accurate information about the budgeting process, assumptions, and adjustments. Transparent communication ensures that stakeholders understand the rationale behind budget decisions and can hold the organization accountable. Accountability involves monitoring actual performance against budgeted targets, identifying and addressing variances, and providing explanations for deviations. Transparent and accountable budgeting practices build trust among stakeholders and enhance organizational integrity.

Responsible Resource Allocation:

Responsible resource allocation is a key ethical consideration in budgeting. Organizations should consider the long, term impact of their budgeting decisions on various stakeholders, including employees, customers, and the community. This entails making choices that align with corporate social responsibility (CSR) principles and contribute positively to society and the environment. Responsible resource allocation involves avoiding unnecessary waste, promoting sustainability, and considering the social and environmental consequences of budgeting decisions.

Ethical Decision, Making Processes:

Ethical decision, making processes are essential in budgeting. Organizations should establish frameworks that incorporate ethical guidelines and promote open dialogue. Ethical decision, making frameworks, such as stakeholder analysis or cost, benefit analysis, can help organizations evaluate the ethical implications of budgeting decisions. Involving key stakeholders in the decision, making process and considering their interests ensures that ethical considerations are integrated into the overall budgeting framework.

Mitigating Conflicts of Interest:

Budgeting processes should address and mitigate conflicts of interest. Individuals involved in budgeting decisions should disclose any personal or financial interests that may influence their decision, making. Organizations should establish policies and procedures to identify, manage, and resolve conflicts of interest to ensure that budgeting decisions are made objectively and in the best interest of the organization and its stakeholders.

Ethical Leadership:

Ethical leadership plays a vital role in promoting ethical considerations in budgeting. Leaders should exemplify integrity, ethical behavior, and a commitment to transparency and fairness. They should communicate and reinforce ethical expectations, provide guidance and support to employees, and create a culture that values ethical decision, making. Ethical leaders promote a shared understanding of ethical principles and empower employees to make ethically sound budgeting decisions.

Regular Ethical Audits and Reviews:

Regular ethical audits and reviews of budgeting processes are crucial to ensure compliance with ethical standards. These audits can be conducted internally or by external parties to evaluate the organization's adherence to ethical principles. Ethical audits examine the integrity of the budgeting process, the accuracy of financial information, and the extent to which ethical considerations are integrated into decision, making. Regular reviews enable organizations to identify areas for improvement and make necessary adjustments to enhance ethical practices.

Promoting Transparency and Accountability in Flexible Budgeting

Promoting Transparency and Accountability in Flexible Budgeting: Fostering Trust and Ethical Practices

Flexible budgeting is a dynamic approach that allows organizations to adapt their budgets to changing circumstances. While the focus is often on the financial benefits and strategic advantages of flexible budgeting, it is equally important to prioritize transparency and accountability in the process. Transparent and accountable budgeting practices build trust among stakeholders and foster ethical behavior. This chapter explores the importance of promoting transparency and accountability in flexible budgeting and highlights key strategies and practices that organizations can implement to ensure ethical and responsible budgeting practices.

Clear Communication and Documentation:

Transparency begins with clear communication and documentation of the budgeting process. Organizations should provide comprehensive explanations of the budgeting process, assumptions, and adjustments made. This includes disclosing the underlying data, methodologies used, and the rationale behind budgeting decisions. Clear communication ensures that stakeholders have a clear understanding of the budgeting process and can provide feedback and input.

Stakeholder Engagement:

Engaging stakeholders in the budgeting process is crucial for promoting transparency and accountability. By involving key stakeholders, such as employees, customers, and shareholders, organizations can gather valuable insights and ensure their perspectives are considered in the budgeting decisions. This involvement can be achieved through regular meetings, surveys, or focus groups, allowing stakeholders to provide input, raise concerns, and contribute to the decision, making process.

Regular Reporting and Disclosure:

Regular reporting and disclosure of budgeting information is essential for fostering transparency and accountability. Organizations should provide timely and accurate reports that outline the actual performance against budgeted targets, highlight variances, and explain the reasons behind deviations. This information should be accessible to all stakeholders, ensuring transparency in the organization's financial activities.

Performance Measurement and Evaluation:

Transparency and accountability are strengthened by establishing performance measurement and evaluation mechanisms. Organizations should define key performance indicators (KPIs) that align with their strategic objectives and budget targets. Regularly monitoring and evaluating performance against these KPIs allows for transparent assessment of budget outcomes and enables proactive decision, making and corrective actions.

Internal Controls and Auditing:

Implementing robust internal controls and conducting regular audits are critical in promoting transparency and accountability. Internal controls help ensure compliance with budgeting policies and procedures, prevent fraud, and provide checks and balances throughout the budgeting process. Independent audits, both internal and external, evaluate the effectiveness of internal controls and verify the accuracy and reliability of financial information.

Ethical Leadership and Tone at the Top:

Ethical leadership sets the tone for promoting transparency and accountability in flexible budgeting. Leaders should demonstrate integrity, lead by example, and foster a culture that values transparency and ethical behavior. Ethical leaders prioritize open communication, encourage questioning and feedback, and create an environment where employees feel comfortable reporting concerns or ethical violations.

Training and Professional Development:

Providing training and professional development opportunities for budgeting personnel is essential for promoting transparency and accountability. Training programs can educate employees on budgeting processes, ethical considerations, data analysis, and reporting standards. This training ensures that budgeting personnel are equipped with the necessary knowledge and skills to carry out their roles ethically and effectively.

Ethical Governance and Oversight:

Establishing ethical governance and oversight mechanisms enhances transparency and accountability in flexible budgeting. This may include creating a budget committee or advisory board responsible for reviewing and approving budget proposals, monitoring budget performance, and ensuring adherence to ethical standards. The committee or board should comprise individuals with diverse expertise and independence to provide objective oversight.

Whistleblower Protection:

Organizations should implement whistleblower protection mechanisms to encourage employees to report any unethical or fraudulent activities related to budgeting. Whistleblower protection policies should ensure confidentiality, provide safeguards against retaliation, and outline a process for investigating and addressing reported concerns.

Ethical Dilemmas in Budget Variance Analysis and Management

Ethical Dilemmas in Budget Variance Analysis and Management: Navigating Challenges in Flexible Budgeting

Budget variance analysis is a crucial component of flexible budgeting, providing valuable insights into the financial performance of an organization. However, this process can present ethical dilemmas that require careful consideration and decision, making. Ethical dilemmas in budget variance analysis often arise from conflicting interests, the interpretation of data, and the potential impact on stakeholders. This chapter explores the ethical dilemmas that can emerge in budget variance analysis and management, particularly in the context of flexible budgeting. It highlights the importance of ethical decision, making and offers strategies for navigating these challenges.

Accuracy and Manipulation of Data:

One ethical dilemma in budget variance analysis is the accuracy and potential manipulation of data. Budget managers may be tempted to manipulate data to present more favorable variances or to meet targets. This can compromise the integrity of the analysis and mislead stakeholders. Ethical decision, making requires adhering to the highest standards of accuracy and transparency when reporting and analyzing variance data. Organizations should establish policies and procedures to ensure data accuracy and implement checks and balances to detect and prevent data manipulation.

Allocating Variances:

Another ethical dilemma in budget variance analysis is the allocation of variances to specific departments or individuals. Variances can be caused by a variety of factors, including external events, unforeseen circumstances, or managerial decisions. Ethical considerations arise when determining who should be held responsible for negative variances. It is important to avoid unfair blame or punishment and instead focus on understanding the root causes of variances and fostering a culture of learning and improvement. Organizations should establish guidelines for allocating variances that are fair, transparent, and based on a thorough analysis of the contributing factors.

Stakeholder Impact:

Budget variance analysis can have a significant impact on various stakeholders, including employees, investors, and customers. Ethical dilemmas arise when the analysis reveals negative variances that may lead to cost, cutting measures, layoffs, or changes in pricing strategies. Balancing the financial interests of the organization with the well, being of stakeholders requires careful consideration and empathy. Ethical decision, making involves engaging with stakeholders, communicating the rationale behind budget decisions, and exploring alternatives that minimize negative impacts on stakeholders while ensuring the organization's sustainability.

Pressure for Short, Term Results:

In some organizations, there may be pressure to achieve short, term financial results, leading to ethical dilemmas in budget variance analysis. Budget managers may face conflicting expectations, such as meeting quarterly targets versus pursuing long, term strategic objectives. Ethical decision, making involves resisting the temptation to prioritize short, term gains over long, term sustainability. Organizations should foster a culture that values ethical behavior, encourages long, term thinking, and supports budget managers in making decisions that align with the organization's values and strategic goals.

Balancing Flexibility and Accountability:

Flexible budgeting allows for adjustments and reallocations of resources based on changing circumstances. However, this flexibility can raise ethical dilemmas regarding accountability. Budget managers may be tempted to use the flexibility of the budget to hide poor performance or avoid accountability for budget variances. Ethical decision, making requires balancing flexibility with accountability. Organizations should establish guidelines and review processes that ensure accountability while allowing for necessary adjustments. This can be achieved through regular performance reviews, transparent reporting, and clear communication of expectations and consequences.

Conflicts of Interest:

Ethical dilemmas in budget variance analysis may also arise from conflicts of interest. Budget managers or decision, makers may have personal interests that conflict with the best interests of the organization. This can lead to biased decision, making, manipulation of data, or favoritism. Organizations should have policies and procedures in place to identify and manage conflicts of interest, ensuring that budgeting decisions are made objectively and in the best interest of the organization and its stakeholders.

Chapter Eighteen

The Psychological Aspects of Flexible Budgeting

The Psychological Aspects of Flexible Budgeting: Understanding the Human Element in Financial Management

Flexible budgeting is a dynamic approach that allows organizations to adjust their budgets in response to changing circumstances. While much emphasis is placed on the financial and strategic aspects of flexible budgeting, it is important to recognize and understand the psychological aspects that come into play. The human element, including individual and group psychology, emotions, biases, and decision, making processes, significantly influences the success of flexible budgeting. This chapter explores the psychological aspects of flexible budgeting and their implications for financial management. It highlights the importance of understanding human behavior and provides insights into how organizations can leverage this understanding to optimize the effectiveness of flexible budgeting.

Cognitive Biases and Decision, Making:

Cognitive biases are inherent in human decision, making processes and can impact the effectiveness of flexible budgeting. Biases such as confirmation bias (the tendency to seek information that confirms preexisting beliefs) or anchoring bias (the reliance on initial information when making decisions) can lead to inaccurate assessments and misjudgments in budgeting. Organizations should be aware of these biases and encourage critical thinking and objective analysis when evaluating budget variances. Implementing mechanisms for independent reviews, brainstorming sessions, and diverse perspectives can help mitigate the influence of cognitive biases.

Emotional Factors and Risk Aversion:

Emotions play a significant role in financial decision, making, including budgeting. Fear, greed, overconfidence, and risk aversion can impact how individuals and groups approach budgeting decisions. For example, individuals may become risk, averse and resistant to adjusting the budget due to fear of failure or loss. Organizations should foster a culture that encourages open dialogue, acknowledges and addresses emotions, and promotes a balanced approach to risk. Providing training and support to enhance emotional intelligence can help individuals and teams navigate these psychological factors more effectively.

Motivation and Incentives:

Motivation is a critical psychological aspect in the context of flexible budgeting. Budgeting processes often involve setting targets and goals, and the way these goals are communicated and incentivized can impact individual and team performance. Organizations should align incentives with the goals of flexible budgeting, promoting behaviors that support adaptability, innovation, and collaboration. Recognizing and rewarding achievements, providing meaningful feedback, and fostering a supportive work environment can enhance motivation and engagement.

Organizational Culture and Communication:

The organizational culture and communication practices significantly influence the psychological aspects of flexible budgeting. A culture that encourages open and transparent communication, collaboration, and learning fosters a positive psychological climate for effective budgeting. Leaders should set the tone by modeling open communication, actively listening to employees, and providing clear expectations. Regularly communicating the purpose and benefits of flexible budgeting, and addressing any concerns or resistance, can help create a culture that embraces change and adaptability.

Collaboration and Team Dynamics:

Flexible budgeting often requires collaboration among different departments and teams. The dynamics of teamwork, including trust, communication, and cooperation, have a profound impact on the success of budgeting processes. Establishing cross, functional teams, encouraging knowledge, sharing, and promoting a sense of shared responsibility can enhance collaboration and enable teams to effectively navigate the complexities of flexible budgeting. Team, building activities and training programs focused on enhancing communication and interpersonal skills can further strengthen teamwork.

Change Management and Employee Engagement:

Implementing flexible budgeting requires managing change effectively and engaging employees throughout the process. Resistance to change is a common psychological response, and organizations should proactively address concerns and provide support. Engaging employees in the decision, making process, providing training and resources, and creating opportunities for input and feedback can help alleviate resistance and foster a sense of ownership and commitment to the flexible budgeting process.

The Impact of Flexible Budgeting on Employee Motivation

The Impact of Flexible Budgeting on Employee Motivation: Empowering Performance and Engagement

Flexible budgeting is a dynamic financial management approach that allows organizations to adjust their budgets in response to changing circumstances. While the benefits of flexible budgeting are often discussed in terms of financial flexibility and decision, making, its impact on employee motivation is equally important. When employees understand and are actively involved in the budgeting process, it can enhance their motivation, performance, and overall engagement. This chapter explores the impact of flexible budgeting on employee motivation and highlights key factors that contribute to a motivated workforce.

Empowering Employees through Involvement:

One of the primary ways flexible budgeting impacts employee motivation is by empowering them through involvement in the budgeting process. When employees have a voice and a role in setting budget targets, identifying cost, saving measures, and making adjustments, they feel a sense of ownership and responsibility. This involvement fosters a deeper understanding of organizational goals and encourages a proactive mindset. Employees are more likely to be motivated when they see their contributions making a difference in achieving budgetary objectives.

Goal Clarity and Alignment:

Flexible budgeting requires clear goal setting and alignment with the overall strategic objectives of the organization. When employees have a clear understanding of these goals and how their work contributes to them, it enhances their sense of purpose and motivation. The budget becomes a tangible representation of these goals, providing employees with a roadmap for their actions and priorities. Clearly communicated budget targets help employees focus their efforts and create a sense of direction and purpose in their work.

Performance Measurement and Recognition:

Flexible budgeting provides a framework for measuring and evaluating performance against budgetary targets. When employees have visibility into their performance in relation to the budget, it creates a sense of accountability and drives motivation. Clear performance metrics and regular feedback help employees gauge their progress and make necessary adjustments. Moreover, when employees achieve or exceed budgetary goals, recognition and rewards further reinforce their motivation and dedication to achieving organizational targets.

Opportunities for Innovation and Problem, Solving:

Flexible budgeting encourages innovation and problem, solving by giving employees the flexibility to explore alternative approaches and solutions. When employees are involved in budgetary discussions, they are more likely to identify inefficiencies, suggest improvements, and propose innovative ideas. This involvement provides a platform for creativity and fosters a culture of continuous improvement. Employees feel motivated when their ideas are valued and implemented, leading to increased job satisfaction and engagement.

Transparency and Trust:

Flexible budgeting promotes transparency and open communication, which are crucial for employee motivation. When employees have access to budget information and understand the rationale behind budgetary decisions, it builds trust and confidence in the organization's management. Transparent communication about budgetary constraints, challenges, and opportunities helps employees see the bigger picture and align their efforts accordingly. Trust and transparency create a positive work environment that fosters motivation and commitment.

Development and Growth Opportunities:

Flexible budgeting can create opportunities for employee development and growth. As employees are involved in budget, related discussions, they gain exposure to financial concepts, strategic thinking, and decision, making processes. This involvement expands their skill set and knowledge base, contributing to their professional growth. Organizations can further support employee development by providing training and educational resources related to budgeting and financial management. Such initiatives enhance employee motivation by demonstrating a commitment to their personal and professional advancement.

Employee Engagement and Collaboration:

Flexible budgeting encourages collaboration and teamwork across departments and teams. This collaborative approach creates a sense of camaraderie and mutual support, fostering employee engagement. When employees work together to achieve budgetary targets, they build stronger relationships and leverage each other's strengths.

Coping with Change: Psychological Factors in Budgeting Flexibility

Budgeting flexibility is essential in today's dynamic business environment, enabling organizations to adapt to changing circumstances and make informed financial decisions. However, the successful implementation of flexible budgeting depends not only on financial strategies but also on understanding the psychological factors that influence individuals' ability to cope with change. This chapter explores the psychological factors that come into play when organizations introduce budgeting flexibility. It emphasizes the importance of addressing these factors to foster a positive mindset and facilitate effective adaptation to changing budgetary requirements.

Change Resistance and Fear:

One of the primary psychological factors that influence individuals' response to budgeting flexibility is the resistance to change. Change can be perceived as disruptive and unsettling, triggering fear and anxiety. Employees may resist new budgeting approaches due to a fear of the unknown or concerns about job security. Organizations should address these concerns by providing clear communication about the need for change, its benefits, and how it aligns with long, term goals. Open dialogue, reassurance, and opportunities for input can help alleviate fear and facilitate a smoother transition to flexible budgeting.

Cognitive Flexibility and Adaptability:

Cognitive flexibility refers to the ability to adapt thinking and behavior in response to new circumstances. It is a key psychological factor that influences how individuals cope with change in budgeting. Those with high cognitive flexibility are more open to new ideas, perspectives, and approaches. Organizations can promote cognitive flexibility by encouraging diverse thinking, providing training on problem, solving and critical thinking skills, and fostering a culture of continuous learning. Developing cognitive flexibility enables individuals to embrace new budgeting methods and navigate evolving financial landscapes.

Communication and Engagement:

Effective communication is crucial in managing psychological factors during the transition to flexible budgeting. Organizations should communicate the rationale behind the change, its benefits, and the role of employees in the process. Engaging employees in decision, making and seeking their input can create a sense of ownership and buy, in. Clear and transparent communication channels, such as town hall meetings, one, on, one discussions, and regular updates, help address concerns, manage expectations, and build trust. Active engagement and involvement foster a sense of control and reduce resistance to change.

Resilience and Adaptation:

Resilience is the ability to bounce back and adapt in the face of adversity or change. In the context of budgeting flexibility, employees need to develop resilience to cope with evolving financial situations. Organizations can support resilience by providing resources for stress management, promoting work, life balance, and offering training programs focused on building emotional resilience. Additionally, recognizing and celebrating small wins throughout the transition process can boost morale and foster a sense of accomplishment, reinforcing resilience and adaptability.

Psychological Safety and Trust:

Psychological safety refers to the belief that one can express ideas, concerns, and questions without fear of negative consequences. It plays a critical role in managing psychological factors during the transition to flexible budgeting. Organizations should create a supportive environment where employees feel safe to voice their opinions, challenge existing practices, and contribute to the development of new budgeting strategies. Building trust through transparent decision, making processes, open dialogue, and empathetic leadership encourages psychological safety and enables individuals to embrace change more effectively.

Learning Orientation and Growth Mindset:

A learning orientation and growth mindset are essential psychological factors for successfully implementing budgeting flexibility. Employees with a learning orientation view challenges as opportunities for growth and improvement. Organizations can promote a growth mindset by providing learning and development opportunities, encouraging experimentation, and recognizing and rewarding learning efforts. Cultivating a learning, oriented culture supports individuals in developing new skills, adapting to new budgeting practices, and embracing change with enthusiasm.

Encouraging a Culture of Adaptability and Innovation

Encouraging a Culture of Adaptability and Innovation: The Key to Successful Flexible Budgeting

In today's rapidly changing business landscape, organizations must embrace adaptability and innovation to stay competitive. This is particularly true when it comes to budgeting practices. Flexible budgeting enables organizations to respond effectively to shifting market conditions and make informed financial decisions. However, the successful implementation of flexible budgeting relies not only on financial strategies but also on cultivating a culture of adaptability and innovation. This chapter explores the importance of fostering such a culture in relation to flexible budgeting and highlights key factors that contribute to its development.

Embracing Change:

A culture of adaptability and innovation begins with a mindset that embraces change. Employees should be encouraged to see change as an opportunity rather than a threat. This can be achieved through effective communication that highlights the benefits of flexible budgeting and the need to adapt to evolving circumstances. By fostering a positive attitude towards change, organizations can create a culture where employees are open to new ideas and eager to explore innovative budgeting approaches.

Empowering Employees:

To encourage adaptability and innovation, employees must feel empowered to contribute their ideas and take ownership of their work. Organizations can foster empowerment by providing autonomy and decision, making authority within budgeting processes. Employees should have the freedom to propose creative solutions, suggest cost, saving measures, and experiment with different approaches. This sense of empowerment not only increases employee engagement but also generates fresh perspectives and innovative ideas.

Promoting Collaboration and Knowledge Sharing:

Collaboration and knowledge sharing are crucial elements of an adaptable and innovative culture. Encouraging cross, functional collaboration allows employees to leverage diverse expertise and experiences. By working together, teams can identify opportunities for process improvement, share best practices, and develop innovative budgeting strategies. This collaborative approach fosters a culture of continuous learning and enhances the organization's ability to adapt to changing circumstances.

Rewarding and Recognizing Innovation:

Innovation should be recognized, celebrated, and rewarded within the organization. This can be done through formal recognition programs, such as innovation awards or bonuses tied to cost, saving initiatives. Recognizing and rewarding innovative ideas and successful implementation of flexible budgeting practices not only motivates employees but also reinforces the organization's commitment to fostering an adaptable and innovative culture.

Providing Resources and Training:

Organizations must provide employees with the necessary resources and training to support their adaptability and innovation. This includes access to relevant technology, data analytics tools, and training programs focused on budgeting techniques and financial management. Equipping employees with the right tools and skills empowers them to embrace flexible budgeting practices and make data, driven decisions that drive innovation.

Encouraging Risk, Taking and Learning from Failure:

A culture of adaptability and innovation requires an environment that encourages risk, taking and learning from failure. Employees should feel supported in taking calculated risks, knowing that their efforts are valued even if the outcome is not always successful. Organizations can foster this culture by promoting experimentation, establishing a safe space for idea generation, and encouraging individuals to learn from both successes and failures. Embracing failure as an opportunity for growth and improvement allows employees to iterate, innovate, and adapt their budgeting strategies.

Leadership Support and Role Modeling:

Leadership plays a vital role in shaping and nurturing a culture of adaptability and innovation. Leaders should actively support and champion flexible budgeting practices, demonstrating their commitment to change and innovation. By setting an example and role modeling adaptive behavior, leaders inspire employees to embrace flexible budgeting and contribute their innovative ideas. Leadership support also ensures that the necessary resources and support are provided to facilitate the implementation of flexible budgeting initiatives.

Chapter Nineteen

Mastering the Art of Flexible Budgeting: Key Takeaways

Flexible budgeting has emerged as a powerful tool for organizations to navigate the complexities of today's business environment. It allows for agility, adaptability, and informed decision, making in response to changing circumstances. As organizations strive to master the art of flexible budgeting, several key takeaways can guide their journey towards success. This chapter explores these takeaways, providing insights into the fundamental principles and best practices that underpin effective flexible budgeting.

Embrace a Forward, Thinking Mindset:

Mastering flexible budgeting begins with adopting a forward, thinking mindset. Recognize that change is inevitable and that budgets must evolve alongside evolving business conditions. Embrace the idea that a budget is not a static document but a dynamic tool that requires continuous assessment and adjustment. By cultivating a forward, thinking mindset, organizations can proactively anticipate and respond to changes, leveraging flexible budgeting to their advantage.

Align Budgeting with Strategic Goals:

A key takeaway in mastering flexible budgeting is the alignment of budgeting activities with strategic goals. Flexible budgets should not be viewed as isolated financial plans but as integral components of an organization's strategic vision. Ensure that budgeting decisions align with broader organizational objectives, enabling the allocation of resources to the most critical areas. This alignment ensures that flexible budgeting supports the overall strategic direction of the organization.

Leverage Accurate and Timely Data:

Accurate and timely data is the lifeblood of effective flexible budgeting. Organizations should invest in robust data collection, analysis, and reporting systems to facilitate informed decision, making. By leveraging accurate and timely data, organizations can identify trends, assess performance against targets, and make proactive adjustments to their budgets. Regular data analysis helps uncover insights and supports evidence, based decision, making in the context of flexible budgeting.

Foster Cross, Functional Collaboration:

Successful flexible budgeting requires collaboration across departments and functions within an organization. Break down silos and foster cross, functional collaboration to ensure that budgeting decisions reflect a holistic view of the organization. By involving stakeholders from various departments, organizations can tap into diverse perspectives and expertise, enhancing the quality of budgeting decisions. Collaborative budgeting processes facilitate knowledge sharing and create a sense of collective ownership.

Continuously Monitor and Evaluate:

Flexibility in budgeting necessitates continuous monitoring and evaluation. Implement mechanisms to track performance against budgeted targets, allowing for timely course corrections. Regular monitoring provides valuable insights into the effectiveness of budgeting strategies and highlights areas where adjustments are required. Emphasize the importance of feedback loops and ensure that evaluation mechanisms are in place to drive ongoing improvement in flexible budgeting practices.

Develop Scenario Planning Capabilities:

Scenario planning is a powerful tool in the arsenal of flexible budgeting. Organizations should develop the capability to model different scenarios and assess their financial implications. By considering a range of possible outcomes, organizations can proactively prepare for various contingencies and mitigate risks. Scenario planning enables organizations to make informed decisions, anticipate potential challenges, and adjust their budgets accordingly.

Communicate and Engage Stakeholders:

Transparent communication and stakeholder engagement are critical in mastering flexible budgeting. Clearly communicate the rationale behind budgeting decisions, the goals being pursued, and the expected outcomes. Engage stakeholders throughout the budgeting process, seeking their input and addressing their concerns. Effective communication and engagement build trust, facilitate buy, in, and create a sense of shared responsibility for the success of flexible budgeting initiatives.

Encourage a Culture of Accountability:

A culture of accountability is a fundamental component of successful flexible budgeting. Foster a culture where individuals and teams take ownership of their budgets, monitor their performance, and take proactive measures to achieve targets. Establish clear accountability frameworks, promote transparency, and celebrate successes that result from responsible budget management.

Lessons Learned from Successful Flexible Budget Implementations

Implementing a flexible budgeting approach can bring numerous benefits to organizations, including improved financial decision, making, adaptability to changing circumstances, and enhanced resource allocation. However, successful implementation requires careful planning, effective execution, and a willingness to learn from past experiences. This chapter explores the lessons learned from successful flexible budget implementations, providing insights into the key factors that contribute to their effectiveness.

Clearly Define Objectives and Scope:

One of the crucial lessons learned is the importance of clearly defining the objectives and scope of the flexible budget implementation. Organizations should establish a clear understanding of why they are adopting a flexible budgeting approach and what they aim to achieve. By setting specific goals and defining the scope of the implementation, organizations can align their efforts and measure success accurately.

Involve Stakeholders from the Start:

Involving stakeholders from the outset is essential for successful flexible budget implementations. Engaging key stakeholders, such as department heads, finance teams, and senior management, fosters a sense of ownership and promotes buy, in throughout the organization. By involving stakeholders in the planning and decision, making processes, organizations can gather valuable insights, address concerns, and build a collaborative approach to flexible budgeting.

Invest in Training and Education:

Successful implementation of flexible budgeting requires investing in training and education for employees involved in the budgeting process. Providing comprehensive training on flexible budgeting concepts, tools, and techniques equips employees with the necessary knowledge and skills to embrace the new approach. This investment ensures that all stakeholders understand the principles of flexible budgeting and can effectively contribute to its implementation.

Develop Clear Processes and Guidelines:

Establishing clear processes and guidelines is critical for a smooth implementation. Organizations should define the steps involved in creating and revising the flexible budget, outline the roles and responsibilities of each stakeholder, and document the decision, making criteria. Clear processes and guidelines ensure consistency and enable effective communication and coordination throughout the budgeting cycle.

Leverage Technology and Automation:

Technology plays a vital role in successful flexible budget implementations. Organizations should leverage budgeting software and automation tools to streamline processes, improve accuracy, and enhance collaboration. These tools enable efficient data collection, analysis, and reporting, saving time and minimizing errors. Technology also facilitates scenario planning, allowing organizations to model different budgeting scenarios and assess their impact.

Foster a Culture of Continuous Learning:

Flexibility requires a culture of continuous learning and improvement. Organizations that embrace a learning mindset and encourage experimentation are better positioned to adapt their budgets to changing circumstances. By fostering a culture that values innovation, encourages feedback, and learns from both successes and failures, organizations can continuously refine their flexible budgeting practices and stay ahead of the curve.

Monitor and Measure Performance:

Monitoring and measuring performance against budgeted targets is a critical aspect of successful flexible budget implementations. Organizations should establish key performance indicators (KPIs) that align with their strategic objectives and regularly track progress. This enables them to identify deviations, understand the reasons behind them, and take corrective actions promptly. Continuous monitoring ensures that budgets remain aligned with organizational goals.

Foster Collaboration and Communication:

Successful flexible budget implementations rely on effective collaboration and communication across departments and levels of the organization. Encouraging open dialogue, sharing best practices, and promoting cross, functional teamwork create an environment where different perspectives can contribute to budgeting decisions. Clear and transparent communication ensures that stakeholders understand the rationale behind budgeting choices and fosters a sense of shared responsibility.

Evaluate and Adjust:

Continuous evaluation and adjustment are key to the long, term success of flexible budgeting. Organizations should regularly assess the effectiveness of their budgeting processes, identify areas for improvement, and make necessary adjustments. Evaluating the impact of flexible budgeting on financial performance and organizational outcomes helps refine strategies and ensures ongoing alignment

Key Skills for Effective Flexible Budgeting

Flexible budgeting is a dynamic approach that requires a specific set of skills to ensure its effectiveness. As organizations strive to embrace this agile budgeting methodology, individuals involved in the process must possess certain key skills. This chapter explores the essential skills for effective flexible budgeting, highlighting their importance in driving accurate financial planning, decision, making, and resource allocation.

Financial Acumen:

A strong foundation in financial acumen is crucial for effective flexible budgeting. Individuals should possess a deep understanding of financial concepts, such as revenue, costs, profit margins, and cash flow. This knowledge allows them to analyze financial data, identify trends, and make informed decisions when creating and adjusting budgets. Financial acumen enables individuals to interpret financial information accurately, ensuring that budgets align with the organization's goals and financial health.

Analytical Skills:

Analytical skills play a vital role in flexible budgeting. Individuals must be proficient in data analysis, capable of examining large datasets, identifying patterns, and drawing meaningful insights. Analytical skills allow for the identification of budget variances, assessing their causes, and making informed decisions regarding budget adjustments. Strong analytical skills help in forecasting future financial scenarios and developing accurate budgeting assumptions.

Communication and Collaboration:

Effective communication and collaboration skills are essential in flexible budgeting. Individuals must be able to effectively convey financial information, explain budgeting processes, and articulate the rationale behind budgeting decisions to stakeholders. Clear and concise communication ensures that everyone understands the objectives, constraints, and expectations of the flexible budgeting approach. Collaboration skills enable individuals to work effectively with cross, functional teams, incorporating diverse perspectives into the budgeting process.

Adaptability and Flexibility:

The ability to adapt to changing circumstances and remain flexible is paramount in flexible budgeting. Individuals must be comfortable with uncertainty and able to adjust their plans and strategies as new information becomes available. They should possess a flexible mindset that embraces change, allowing for quick decision, making and resource reallocation when necessary. Adaptability ensures that budgets remain relevant and aligned with the organization's evolving needs and goals.

Problem, Solving:

Effective flexible budgeting requires strong problem, solving skills. Individuals should be adept at identifying budgeting challenges, analyzing their root causes, and developing practical solutions. Problem, solving skills enable individuals to address budget variances, inefficiencies, and bottlenecks effectively. They can proactively identify opportunities for cost savings, revenue enhancement, and process improvements. Strong problem, solving skills contribute to the continuous improvement of flexible budgeting practices.

Strategic Thinking:

Strategic thinking is a critical skill for effective flexible budgeting. Individuals must have a big, picture perspective, understanding the organization's strategic goals and aligning budgeting decisions accordingly. They should be able to evaluate the long, term implications of budgeting choices, assess the potential risks and opportunities, and make decisions that support the organization's overall strategy. Strategic thinking ensures that flexible budgets are not created in isolation but as integral parts of the organization's strategic framework.

Attention to Detail:

Attention to detail is crucial in flexible budgeting to ensure accuracy and precision. Individuals must have a keen eye for detail when collecting, analyzing, and reporting financial data. Even minor errors or omissions can have a significant impact on budgeting outcomes. Attention to detail helps individuals identify discrepancies, reconcile data, and maintain the integrity of the budgeting process. Diligence in reviewing budget assumptions and double, checking calculations is essential for reliable budgeting results.

Time Management:

Effective time management is a valuable skill in flexible budgeting. Individuals must be able to prioritize tasks, meet deadlines, and manage competing demands effectively. Time management skills ensure that budgeting activities are conducted in a timely manner, enabling timely decision, making and adjustments.

The Future of Budgeting: Staying Flexible in a Changing World

Budgeting has long been a cornerstone of financial management, providing organizations with a roadmap for allocating resources and achieving their goals. However, in today's fast, paced and unpredictable business landscape, traditional budgeting approaches are facing increasing challenges. As organizations navigate through economic uncertainties, technological advancements, and evolving customer demands, the need for flexible budgeting becomes paramount. This chapter explores the future of budgeting and the importance of staying flexible in a changing world, highlighting how flexible budgeting can help organizations thrive in dynamic environments.

Embracing Agility:

In a rapidly changing world, organizations must adopt an agile mindset when it comes to budgeting. The traditional annual budgeting process, with its fixed targets and rigid assumptions, is no longer sufficient. Instead, organizations should embrace flexible budgeting, which allows for real, time adjustments and course corrections. By regularly reviewing and updating budgets based on changing market conditions and internal dynamics, organizations can respond quickly to new opportunities or challenges, ensuring resource allocation aligns with strategic priorities.

Leveraging Technology:

Technology plays a crucial role in the future of budgeting. Advanced software applications and data analytics enable organizations to gather and process large volumes of financial data efficiently. With real, time insights into revenue, costs, and performance metrics, organizations can make informed decisions and adjust budgets accordingly. Furthermore, technology allows for scenario modeling and predictive analysis, helping organizations anticipate future financial outcomes and develop contingency plans. The integration of technology with flexible budgeting enhances decision, making and improves overall financial management.

Data, Driven Decision Making:

The future of budgeting is increasingly reliant on data, driven decision, making processes. Organizations are leveraging big data and analytics to gain deeper insights into customer behavior, market trends, and competitive dynamics. By harnessing this wealth of information, organizations can make more accurate revenue and cost projections, identify growth opportunities, and optimize resource allocation. Data, driven decision, making enables organizations to align their budgets with market realities, improving the accuracy and effectiveness of their financial planning.

Continuous Planning and Forecasting:

In a rapidly changing world, traditional annual budgeting cycles may be insufficient to capture the nuances of evolving business environments. Instead, organizations are shifting towards continuous planning and forecasting processes. This approach involves regular reviews and updates to budgets based on real, time data and market insights. Continuous planning allows organizations to adapt their strategies and resource allocation dynamically, taking advantage of emerging opportunities and mitigating potential risks. By continuously monitoring performance and adjusting budgets, organizations can stay ahead of the curve and maintain a competitive edge.

Integrated Financial and Operational Planning:

The future of budgeting lies in the integration of financial and operational planning. Traditionally, these two functions have operated in silos, resulting in misalignment and inefficiencies. By integrating financial and operational planning processes, organizations can ensure that budgets reflect operational realities and strategic goals. This approach enables organizations to better understand the financial implications of operational decisions, identify areas for cost optimization, and allocate resources effectively. Integrated planning facilitates a holistic view of the organization, enabling better decision, making and driving overall performance.

Enhanced Risk Management:

Flexibility in budgeting goes hand in hand with effective risk management. In a changing world, organizations face a myriad of risks, ranging from economic volatility to cybersecurity threats. Flexible budgeting allows organizations to incorporate risk management considerations into their financial planning processes. By conducting scenario analysis and stress testing, organizations can assess the potential impact of risks on their budgets and develop contingency plans. By proactively managing risks and integrating risk considerations into budgeting, organizations can enhance their resilience and ensure financial sustainability.

Chapter Twenty

Final Thoughts: Developing a Flexible Mindset

Embracing Adaptability: Developing a Flexible Mindset

Flexible budgeting is a dynamic approach that empowers organizations to navigate changing circumstances, optimize resource allocation, and drive financial success. However, the effectiveness of flexible budgeting is not solely dependent on tools and techniques—it also requires a flexible mindset. Developing a flexible mindset is essential for organizations to embrace change, adapt to new realities, and make informed decisions in a rapidly evolving business landscape. Below we will explore the importance of developing a flexible mindset in relation to flexible budgeting and discuss key strategies to foster adaptability and agility within organizations.

Embrace a Growth Mindset:

Developing a flexible mindset begins with adopting a growth mindset—a belief that abilities and intelligence can be developed through dedication and effort. Embracing a growth mindset encourages individuals and organizations to view challenges as opportunities for growth and learning. In the context of flexible budgeting, a growth mindset allows for open, mindedness, curiosity, and a willingness to explore new approaches. It promotes a culture of continuous improvement, where mistakes are seen as learning opportunities and feedback is welcomed. By fostering a growth mindset, organizations can cultivate an environment that encourages flexibility and adaptability in budgeting processes.

Foster Collaboration and Communication:

Flexible budgeting requires collaboration and effective communication among stakeholders. Developing a flexible mindset involves breaking down silos and promoting cross, functional collaboration. Encouraging open and transparent communication channels enables the exchange of ideas, diverse perspectives, and collective problem, solving. By fostering collaboration and communication, organizations can gather valuable insights, challenge assumptions, and adapt budgeted amounts based on a broader understanding of the business landscape. Effective collaboration promotes flexibility, enhances decision, making, and drives better financial outcomes.

Encourage Continuous Learning:

To develop a flexible mindset, organizations must foster a culture of continuous learning. This involves encouraging employees to acquire new knowledge, develop new skills, and stay updated on industry trends and best practices. Continuous learning enables individuals to adapt to changing circumstances, explore innovative approaches, and embrace emerging technologies. Organizations can facilitate continuous learning by providing training programs, promoting knowledge, sharing initiatives, and supporting professional development opportunities. By investing in continuous learning, organizations equip their employees with the skills and knowledge needed to navigate complex budgeting challenges and embrace flexibility.

Promote Risk, Taking and Experimentation:

Developing a flexible mindset requires a willingness to take risks and experiment with new ideas. Organizations should create a safe environment that encourages calculated risk, taking and innovation. This involves empowering employees to challenge the status quo, propose new budgeting approaches, and test innovative solutions. By promoting risk, taking and experimentation, organizations can uncover new insights, discover more efficient processes, and identify opportunities for improvement. Embracing a culture of innovation and experimentation fosters adaptability, encourages flexibility, and supports the evolution of budgeting practices.

Emphasize Data, Driven Decision, Making:

A flexible mindset is rooted in data, driven decision, making. Organizations should encourage the use of data and analytics to inform budgeting decisions. This involves leveraging big data, advanced analytics tools, and performance metrics to gain insights into financial performance, market trends, and customer behavior. By basing budgeting decisions on reliable data, organizations can ensure that budgeted amounts are aligned with strategic goals and market realities. Data, driven decision, making promotes objectivity, enhances accuracy, and enables organizations to adapt their budgeted amounts based on empirical evidence.

Embrace Change as an Opportunity:

Finally, developing a flexible mindset requires embracing change as an opportunity rather than a threat. In a rapidly evolving business landscape, organizations must anticipate and embrace change, rather than resist it. This involves encouraging employees to be adaptable, agile, and open to new possibilities. Organizations can create a culture that celebrates innovation, embraces change, and rewards creative problem, solving.

The Benefits of a Flexible Approach to Budgeting

Unleashing Potential: The Benefits of a Flexible Approach to Budgeting

Budgeting is a fundamental process that organizations use to plan, allocate resources, and monitor financial performance. Traditionally, budgeting has been a static exercise, focused on fixed plans and rigid allocations. However, in today's fast, paced and unpredictable business environment, organizations are increasingly recognizing the value of a flexible approach to budgeting. Flexible budgeting allows for adjustments and adaptations in response to changing circumstances, enabling organizations to optimize resource allocation and drive financial success. Below we will explore the benefits of a flexible approach to budgeting and discuss how organizations can leverage these advantages to enhance their financial management practices.

Adaptability to Changing Circumstances:

One of the key benefits of a flexible approach to budgeting is the ability to adapt to changing circumstances. In today's dynamic business environment, organizations face numerous factors that can impact their financial performance, including market fluctuations, customer demands, and technological advancements. A flexible budget allows organizations to adjust budgeted amounts based on the latest information and changing circumstances. This adaptability enables organizations to allocate resources more effectively, seize new opportunities, and mitigate risks. By embracing flexibility, organizations can ensure that their budgeted amounts remain relevant and aligned with the evolving needs of the business.

Optimal Resource Allocation:

Flexible budgeting facilitates optimal resource allocation by aligning budgets with organizational priorities and performance targets. Traditional budgeting often relied on fixed allocations that may not reflect the current needs of the organization. A flexible budget, on the other hand, enables organizations to reallocate resources based on actual activity levels or changes in business operations. This dynamic allocation of resources ensures that scarce resources are directed to areas that generate the most value and contribute to organizational goals. By optimizing resource allocation, organizations can enhance productivity, reduce waste, and achieve better financial outcomes.

Improved Decision, Making:

A flexible approach to budgeting promotes improved decision, making by providing timely and relevant information. Traditional budgeting processes often involve long planning cycles and static plans that may not reflect the latest market conditions or customer demands. In contrast, a flexible budget allows organizations to make informed decisions based on real, time information and up, to, date financial data. This agility in decision, making enables organizations to respond quickly to emerging opportunities or challenges, adjust budgeted amounts as needed, and allocate resources strategically. By incorporating flexibility into budgeting, organizations can make more accurate, timely, and effective decisions, driving financial success.

Enhanced Performance Evaluation:

Flexible budgeting enhances performance evaluation by providing a more accurate assessment of financial performance. Traditional budgeting often relied on a fixed budget that may not reflect the actual activity levels or changes in the business environment. As a result, comparing actual results to the fixed budget may not provide an accurate measure of performance. Flexible budgeting, on the other hand, allows organizations to compare actual results to budgeted amounts adjusted for the actual activity levels achieved. This provides a more realistic evaluation of performance, enabling organizations to identify areas of improvement, address budget variances, and make informed decisions for future planning. By adopting a flexible approach to budgeting, organizations can enhance performance evaluation and drive continuous improvement.

Agility in Response to Uncertainties:

A flexible budgeting approach enables organizations to navigate uncertainties and adapt to unforeseen circumstances. In today's volatile business environment, organizations face a wide range of uncertainties, such as economic fluctuations, regulatory changes, or unexpected market disruptions. A flexible budget allows organizations to anticipate and respond to these uncertainties by adjusting budgeted amounts accordingly. This agility enables organizations to mitigate the impact of external shocks, seize new opportunities, and maintain financial stability. By embracing flexibility, organizations can proactively respond to uncertainties and position themselves for long, term success.

The Link Between Flexible Budgeting and Organizational Culture

Nurturing Adaptability: The Link Between Flexible Budgeting and Organizational Culture

Organizational culture plays a crucial role in shaping the mindset, values, and behaviors within an organization. It influences how employees approach their work, make decisions, and collaborate. Flexible budgeting, on the other hand, is a dynamic approach that allows organizations to adapt to changing circumstances and optimize resource allocation. The link between flexible budgeting and organizational culture is vital, as a supportive culture promotes the successful implementation of flexible budgeting practices. Below we will explore the link between flexible budgeting and organizational culture, highlighting how a culture that embraces adaptability and collaboration enhances the effectiveness of flexible budgeting.

Embracing Change and Adaptability:

Flexible budgeting requires organizations to embrace change and adaptability, and this is closely tied to the organization's culture. A culture that encourages openness, innovation, and adaptability provides a fertile ground for the successful implementation of flexible budgeting practices. When employees are encouraged to question the status quo, explore new ideas, and adapt to changing circumstances, they are more likely to embrace the dynamic nature of flexible budgeting. A culture that values adaptability encourages employees to challenge traditional budgeting practices, experiment with new approaches, and seek continuous improvement in financial management processes.

Encouraging Collaboration and Communication:

Collaboration and communication are essential components of both flexible budgeting and a positive organizational culture. Flexible budgeting requires input and collaboration from various stakeholders across different departments or functions. An organizational culture that fosters collaboration and effective communication facilitates the sharing of information, perspectives, and insights necessary for successful flexible budgeting. When employees feel comfortable sharing ideas, seeking feedback, and working together, it promotes a culture of transparency and knowledge exchange, enhancing the effectiveness of flexible budgeting practices.

Empowering Decision, Making at All Levels:

Flexible budgeting encourages empowered decision, making at all levels of the organization. It involves empowering employees to take ownership of budgeting decisions, contribute their expertise, and make informed choices based on the organization's goals and priorities. An organizational culture that values employee empowerment and decentralized decision, making provides the foundation for successful flexible budgeting. When employees are trusted and empowered to make decisions within their areas of responsibility, it promotes accountability, creativity, and agility in budgeting processes.

Promoting a Learning Culture:

A learning culture is closely linked to the success of flexible budgeting. Organizations that prioritize learning and development create an environment where employees are encouraged to acquire new knowledge, develop new skills, and stay updated on industry trends. A learning culture supports the implementation of flexible budgeting by fostering a mindset of continuous improvement and adaptability. When employees are encouraged to seek new information, challenge assumptions, and apply new techniques, they are better equipped to navigate the complexities of flexible budgeting and embrace change.

Aligning Values and Goals:

Organizational culture shapes the values and goals of an organization. When the values and goals align with the principles of flexible budgeting, it creates a strong link between the two. For example, if an organization values innovation, efficiency, and customer, centricity, it is more likely to embrace flexible budgeting practices that support these principles. An organizational culture that emphasizes the importance of strategic resource allocation, financial accountability, and responsiveness to market changes is conducive to the implementation of flexible budgeting. When the culture and the budgeting approach align, it enhances the organization's ability to adapt, achieve financial targets, and drive long, term success.

Leadership and Role Modeling:

Organizational culture is significantly influenced by leadership behaviors and role modeling. Leaders play a crucial role in shaping the culture of an organization and creating an environment that supports flexible budgeting.

Ensuring Long

,

Term Success with Flexible Budgeting

Thriving in a Dynamic Environment: Ensuring Long, Term Success with Flexible Budgeting

Flexible budgeting is a powerful tool that enables organizations to adapt to changing circumstances, optimize resource allocation, and drive financial success. However, to ensure long, term success with flexible budgeting, organizations need to adopt a holistic approach that encompasses various factors. It involves aligning the budgeting process with strategic goals, fostering a supportive organizational culture, leveraging technology, and embracing continuous improvement. Below we will explore key strategies to ensure long, term success with flexible budgeting and discuss how organizations can navigate challenges and capitalize on opportunities for sustained financial excellence.

Aligning Budgeting with Strategic Goals:

To ensure long, term success, organizations must align their budgeting process with strategic goals. Flexible budgeting should reflect the priorities, objectives, and vision of the organization. By integrating strategic goals into the budgeting process, organizations can allocate resources in a manner that supports the overall direction of the business. This alignment ensures that budgeted amounts are allocated to critical initiatives, growth areas, and value, added activities. By consistently evaluating the strategic alignment of the budget, organizations can ensure that their flexible budgets drive long, term success.

Fostering a Culture of Adaptability:

A supportive organizational culture is vital for long, term success with flexible budgeting. Organizations should foster a culture that values adaptability, innovation, and continuous learning. Employees should be encouraged to embrace change, challenge assumptions, and contribute their insights to the budgeting process. A culture that embraces adaptability fosters agility, resilience, and creativity in budgeting practices. By nurturing a culture of adaptability, organizations can better navigate uncertainties, respond to market changes, and make informed decisions that drive long, term success.

Leveraging Technology:

In today's digital era, technology plays a pivotal role in enhancing the effectiveness of flexible budgeting. Organizations should leverage technology to streamline the budgeting process, enhance data accuracy, and enable real, time monitoring and analysis. Budgeting software and advanced analytics tools can automate routine tasks, provide accurate financial information, and generate insights to inform decision, making. By embracing technology, organizations can improve the efficiency of the budgeting process, enhance data, driven decision, making, and ensure that flexible budgets are based on reliable information for long, term success.

Implementing Robust Performance Measurement:

Robust performance measurement is essential for long, term success with flexible budgeting. Organizations should establish key performance indicators (KPIs) and metrics that align with strategic goals and monitor them regularly. By tracking performance against these metrics, organizations can evaluate the effectiveness of their flexible budgets, identify areas for improvement, and make informed adjustments. Performance measurement enables organizations to assess the impact of budgeting decisions, identify trends, and take corrective actions to drive long, term success.

Encouraging Cross, Functional Collaboration:

Cross, functional collaboration is critical for long, term success with flexible budgeting. Budgeting decisions often require inputs and involvement from various departments and stakeholders within the organization. Organizations should encourage collaboration and communication across functions to foster a holistic understanding of the budgeting process. By involving key stakeholders from different areas, organizations can leverage diverse perspectives, mitigate information silos, and ensure that budgeted amounts reflect the needs and realities of the entire organization. Cross, functional collaboration enhances the effectiveness of flexible budgeting and facilitates buy, in from all stakeholders for long, term success.

Embracing Continuous Improvement:

Continuous improvement is a key principle for long, term success with flexible budgeting. Organizations should foster a culture of learning, innovation, and continuous improvement in the budgeting process. This involves conducting regular reviews and evaluations of the budgeting process to identify areas for enhancement. By seeking feedback, analyzing outcomes, and identifying best practices, organizations can refine their flexible budgeting practices over time.

9781776846962

SD - #0034 - 140926 - C0 - 229/152/13 - PB - 9781776846962 - Matt Lamination